Superstars

This edition first published in 1998 by
PRC Publishing Ltd,
Kiln House, 210 New Kings Road, London SW6 4NZ

ISBN 1 85648 490 4

Printed and bound in Spain

Acknowledgements
Sue Heady would like to thank John Haylett at 'Ace', Alan Hepburn, the ATP and WTA press offices, and the
Wimbledon Lawn Tennis Museum for all their help.

Andre Agassi

STATISTICS

Date of Birth: April 29, 1970
Place of Birth: Las Vegas, Nevada, USA
Place of Residence: Las Vegas, Nevada, USA
Nationality: US
Height: 5ft 11in (1.80m)
Plays: Right-handed
Highest Ranking Reached: No. 1 (April 10, 1995)

Career Title Wins
Singles: 34
Doubles: 1

Grand Slam Highlights
Singles
Australian—won 1995; SF 1996
French—runner-up 1990, 1991; SF 1988, 1992; QF 1995
Wimbledon—won 1992; SF 1995; QF 1991, 1993
US—won 1994; runner-up 1990, 1995; SF 1988, 1989, 1996; QF 1992

Awards
ATP Tour Most Improved Player 1988
ATP Tour Humanitarian of the Year 1995

Thanks to his flamboyant appearance and exciting tennis, Agassi is credited by many with reviving interest in tennis worldwide.

In a sport that is often accused of being boring and its players bland, Agassi has always attracted attention, thanks to his denim shorts, fluorescent coloured T-shirts, wraparound shades, bandanas worn pirate-style and different haircuts (one moment long peroxide blonde, the next shaven). More recent accessories, such as his personal 727 jet and his wife, Hollywood star Brooke Shields, have further added to his rock 'n' roll appeal, making him one of the United States' great sporting superstars.

That, however, is to detract from his tennis, which can be—if Agassi is concentrated and on form—of the highest level. Like John McEnroe, Agassi has fantastic hand-eye coordination, which allows him to take the ball very early and to hit it very hard. This is most obvious when he whips a return off either flank. He certainly doesn't wait for his opponents to make mistakes, he'd rather go for a winner every time.

A natural since he picked up his first ball at the age of four, Agassi went to the famous Nick Bollettieri Tennis Academy in Florida at the age of 14. Two years later, he emerged as a bright young star on the ATP Tour and, in 1987, won his first title as a wild card entrant in Itaparica. He made it to the finals of the French Open in 1990 and 1991, and the US Open in 1990, but it was not until Wimbledon 1992, playing only his 13th game on grass, that Agassi finally fulfilled his prodigious talent and won a Grand Slam.

Since then, he has had his ups and downs. After parting company with his mentor, Bollettieri, there were times when he appeared to find it hard to balance his personal and professional lives. Still, under the guidance of former professional Brad Gilbert, he managed to win another two Grand Slams— the US Open in 1994 and the 1995 Australian Open.

In 1997, Agassi had his least successful year on the Tour since turning pro and dropped to No. 141 in the rankings. Just as his critics were beginning to doubt that he would ever return to his best form, Agassi announced 'the siesta is over' and returned to his winning ways.

In February 1998, he won the Sybase Open in San Jose, with a final, straight sets victory over world No. 1 Pete Sampras. Agassi, it would appear, is well on the road to recovery.

Arthur Ashe

STATISTICS

Date of Birth: July 10, 1943
Place of Birth: Richmond, Virginia, USA
Date of Death: February 6, 1993
Nationality: US
Height: 5ft 11in (1.81m)
Played: Right-handed
Highest Ranking Reached: No. 2 (May 10, 1976)

Career Title Wins
Singles: 33
Doubles: 18

Grand Slam Highlights
Singles
Australian—won 1970; runner-up 1971; SF 1978; QF 1977

French—QF 1971
Wimbledon—won 1975; SF 1968, 1969
US—won 1968; runner-up 1972; SF 1969, 1971; QF 1970, 1974

Doubles
Australian—won (w/Roche) 1977
French—won (w/Riessen) 1971; runner-up (w/Pasarell) 1970
Wimbledon—runner-up (w/Ralston) 1971
US—runner-up (w/Gimeno) 1968

Awards
ATP Tour Player of the Year 1975
ATP Tour Sportsmanship Award 1977
ATP Tour Comeback Player of the Year 1979
ATP Tour Humanitarian of the Year 1992

Arthur Ashe is the only black male to have won a Grand Slam singles title—and he has three of them. The only other black player to have come close to winning one is compatriot MaliVai Washington, who reached the finals of the Wimbledon's men's event in 1996.

Ashe came from humble beginnings. He grew up in Richmond, Virginia, in the days of racial segregation, which meant that he was banned from mainstream junior tournaments. Dr Walter Johnson, who had previously helped the black tennis star Althea Gibson, ensured that Ashe finished high school in St Louis, where he was allowed to play competitions.

In the 1960s, Ashe attended the University of California at Los Angeles. In 1963, he became the first black to be selected for American Davis Cup duty and, two years later, won the US Intercollegiate singles.

Despite being a finalist at the Australian Championships in 1966 and 1967, Ashe did not turn professional at the start of the open era in 1968. He retained his amateur status so that he could still play Davis Cup and gain leave from the US Army (he was doing his

national service at the time) to play tournaments. As a result, Ashe managed to win both the US Amateur and the US Open events in 1968—the first and only time that a player is likely to do so.

He was to win another two major titles: the Australian Open in 1970 and Wimbledon in 1975. The latter was a stunning upset over Jimmy Connors, who was the 10-1 favourite. In a true case of brains over brawn, Ashe (who meditated during changeovers!) beat the top seed 6-1, 6-1, 5-7, 6-4.

In 1976, the year that Ashe finally made the No. 1 ranking, he suffered an Achilles heel injury and was forced to miss most of the 1977 season. He staged a comeback in 1978, but, in July 1979, suffered a heart attack and had to undergo triple bypass surgery, which effectively ended his playing career.

Ashe remained involved in tennis. He was the US Davis Cup captain from 1980 to 1985, and also worked as a journalist and television commentator. In 1992, however, he revealed that he had contracted the AIDS virus through a blood transfusion. He died the following year.

Tracy Austin

STATISTICS

Date of Birth: December 12, 1962
Place of Birth: Palos Verdes Peninsula, California, USA
Place of Residence: Rolling Rocks, California, USA
Nationality: US
Height: 5ft 5in (1.65m)
Plays: Right-handed
Highest Ranking Reached: No. 1 (April 7, 1980)

Career Title Wins
Singles: 29
Doubles: 4

Grand Slam Highlights
Singles
Australian—QF 1981
French—QF 1982, 1983
Wimbledon—SF 1979, 1980; QF 1981, 1982
US—won 1979, 1981; SF 1980; QF 1977, 1978, 1982

Mixed Doubles
Wimbledon—won (w/Austin) 1980

Awards
WTA Most Impressive Newcomer 1977
WTA Player of the Year 1980

Tracy Austin was born into a tennis playing family—with her brother John, she won the Wimbledon mixed doubles title in 1980 (the only brother/sister pairing ever to do so).

Austin was winning tournaments from a very young age. In 1972, she won her first major junior event, the US National 12s title, at the age of just 10. She then went on to capture 25 US Nationals' junior titles—the most ever won by a boy or girl.

In 1977, at 14 years and 28 days, Austin won her first professional event. Later in the year, she became the youngest player at Wimbledon for 70 years. She appeared on numerous front pages, in her trademark bunches, braces and pinafore dresses, and was interviewed endlessly by feature writers. Austin was used to the attention—she had first appeared as a cover girl, on the front of *World Tennis*, at the age of four.

At the US Open later that year, Austin, an unseeded amateur, reached the quarter-finals, beating Britain's Sue Barker and the Italian Virginia Ruzici en route. She was, until Jennifer Capriati stole her crown, the youngest Grand Slam quarter-finalist, but must still rank as the smallest at a height of just 5ft and a weight of only 90lb.

Austin may have been beaten by Martina Navratilova in the fourth round of the main draw at Wimbledon in 1978, but she still won the girls' event, beating Hana Mandlikova in a three-set final.

In 1979, Austin won the US Open, beating Chris Evert 6-4, 6-3 and becoming the youngest ever champion. Two years later, she defeated the other grand dame of ladies' tennis, Navratilova, to take the US Open title once again.

Despite her slight build, her patience, perseverance and ground strokes (particularly her deadly passing shots from the baseline) gave her an edge over most players. For six years, between 1978 and 1983, she had a top ten ranking and twice, albeit briefly, she was No. 1, breaking the stranglehold that Evert and Navratilova had on the top spot for many years.

Unfortunately, sciatic back problems began to hinder Austin's progress in the early 1980s. She won her last professional title in 1982 and effectively retired from the game before she turned 21. She tried to return to the Tour on several occasions (in 1988, she reached the US Open mixed doubles semi-finals), but—particularly after a serious car accident in 1989—never achieved great success.

Boris Becker

STATISTICS

Date of Birth: November 22, 1967
Place of Birth: Leimen, Germany
Place of Residence: Munich, Germany
Nationality: German
Height: 6ft 3in (1.90m)
Plays: Right-handed
Highest Ranking Reached: No. 1 (January 28, 1991)

Career Title Wins
Singles: 49
Doubles: 15

Grand Slam Highlights
Singles
Australian—won 1991, 1996; QF 1984, 1990
French—SF 1987, 1989, 1991; QF 1986
Wimbledon—won 1985, 1986, 1989; runner-up 1988, 1990, 1991, 1995; SF 1993, 1994; QF 1992, 1997
US—won 1989; SF 1986, 1990, 1995

Awards
ATP Most Improved Player of the Year 1985
ATP Player of the Year 1989

Boris Becker enjoyed a meteoric rise to fame. At the end of 1983, he was ranked No. 563 in the world. Eighteen months later, he beat South Africa's Kevin Curren to become the only unseeded player, the youngest player and the first German to win the men's singles title at Wimbledon.

Becker's success relied heavily on his powerful forehand, diving volleys and booming serves, which were particularly lethal on grass. The tabloid press subsequently nicknamed him 'Boom Boom Becker', a sobriquet which could easily have applied to the impact that his success had on the German tennis scene.

Thanks to him (and helped, a few years later, by Steffi Graf), the membership of the German tennis federation doubled between 1985 and 1993, and the number of hours of tennis broadcast on German television rose from 13 in 1984 to 2,673 in 1993.

As a child, Becker played both tennis and football, but he gave up the latter in favour of tennis at the age of 12. He was fortunate in that he lived in Leimen, a small town in south-west Germany which has a well-established tennis centre. It was there, too, that Steffi Graf, Anke Huber and a host of other of today's Tour players trained in their formative years.

As a professional, Becker was guided by Ion Tiriac, the former Romanian tennis star. Under his tutelage, the young German won Wimbledon again, in 1986 and 1989, the US Open in 1989 and the Australian Open in 1991—the latter pushing his ranking up into the No. 1 spot.

Soon after, Becker split with Tiriac and experienced a period of angst, when the press labelled him 'the thinker' because he always seemed to have something to say about the homeless, the environment, racism . . . everything, in fact, but tennis.

However, marriage at the end of 1993, shortly followed by the arrival of a son, appeared to calm Becker and he returned to form. In 1994, he won the Stockholm Open, achieving a rare feat: he beat the world's top three players—No. 1 Pete Sampras (SF), No. 2 Croatia's Goran Ivanisevic (F) and No. 3 compatriot Michael Stich (QF)—in one tournament. The following year, he reached the final at Wimbledon (losing to Sampras, who was winning for the third time) and in 1996 once again won the Australian Open.

In 1997, having been beaten by Sampras in the Wimbledon quarter-finals, Becker announced that he would no longer play the Grand Slams. These days, he only participates in selected Tour events.

Bjorn Borg

STATISTICS

Date of Birth: June 6, 1956
Place of Birth: Sodertalje, Sweden
Place of Residence: Monte Carlo, Monaco
Nationality: Swedish
Height: 5ft 11in (1.80m)
Plays: Right-handed
Highest Ranking Reached: No. 1 (August 23, 1977)

Career Title Wins
Singles: 62
Doubles: 4

Grand Slam Highlights
Singles
French—won 1974, 1975, 1978, 1979, 1980, 1981; QF 1976
Wimbledon—won 1976, 1977, 1978, 1979, 1980; runner-up 1981; QF 1973, 1975
US—runner-up 1976, 1978, 1980, 1981; QF 1979

Awards
ATP Tour Player of the Year 1976, 1977, 1978, 1979, 1980

Very few players have made a lasting impression on tennis: Bjorn Borg is one of them. He will always be remembered for his great skills, unfailing sportsmanship and remarkably ice-cool on-court demeanour, as well as for being the inspiration for a generation of Swedish players.

His records, which still stand today, are impressive. He has won the most Grand Slam singles titles and the most consecutive Wimbledon titles (five) in the open era, as well as the most consecutive (four) and total number of French Open titles (six) in history. What is more, Borg won them all before he retired at the tender age of 26.

When Borg was still a youngster, his father won a tennis racquet in a table tennis tournament. He gave it to his son and a great career was born. In 1973, as a 17-year-old, he burst on to the professional scene with a quarter-final finish at Wimbledon.

Less than a year later, he won the French Open. Borg's patient, baseline game was perfectly suited to clay. His heavy topspin ground strokes, including (unusually for a man at that time) a double-fisted backhand, were extremely effective and, together with his great strength and endurance, won him many matches.

But Borg, having won the boys' singles at Wimbledon in 1972, knew that he could also win on grass. So for two weeks prior to the 1976 Championships, he practised serving and volleying. His determination, and talent, paid off. He won the men's singles title without the loss of a set.

It was the first of five successive titles. The most memorable final, which has long been written into the history books as a classic, was against John McEnroe in 1980, when Borg won 1-6, 7-5, 6-3, 6-7 (16-18), 8-6 in just under three hours, the fourth set tiebreak being particularly dramatic.

Unfortunately, the winning could not continue for ever. In the 1981 Wimbledon final, McEnroe finally dethroned Borg and, to add salt to the wound, beat him in the US Open finals later in the year. The defeat in America knocked Borg off the No. 1 spot and, soon after, he decided to retire.

Failed business ventures forced the Swede to make a comeback in 1991. He played eight singles and three doubles events, but found it hard to win. A switch to the Senior ATP Tour in 1993 met with greater success. His outside business interests, which now include an underwear company, also appear to have picked up.

Jennifer Capriati

STATISTICS

Date of Birth: March 29, 1976
Place of Birth: New York, New York, USA
Place of Residence: Wesley Chapel, Florida, USA
Nationality: US
Height: 5ft 8.5in (1.74m)
Plays: Right-handed
Highest Ranking Reached: No. 6 (September 9, 1991)

Career Title Wins
Singles: 6
Doubles: 1

Grand Slam Highlights
Singles
Australian—QF 1992, 1993
French—SF 1990; QF 1992, 1993
Wimbledon—SF 1991; QF 1992, 1993
US—SF 1991

Mixed Doubles
Wimbledon—QF (w/Jensen) 1992

Awards
WTA Tour Most Impressive Newcomer 1990
WTA Tour Comeback Player of the Year 1996

In 1990, Jennifer Capriati arrived on the women's tennis tour amid much hype—and US$5 million worth of endorsements before she had even played a point. With her bubbly, youthful personality off court and her thirst for demolishing older, more experienced players on court, Capriati was a welcome breath of fresh air.

In Boca Raton, at her first tournament as a pro, she defeated five opponents (including France's Nathalie Tauziat and the Czech Helena Sukova), before losing to Gabriela Sabatini 6-4, 7-5 in the final.

She then went on to amass an incredible number of milestones. At the age of 14, at the 1990 French Open, she became the youngest Grand Slam semi-finalist in tennis history— she lost to eventual tournament champion Monica Seles. A few weeks later, she was the youngest seed (No. 12) in Grand Slam history at Wimbledon, where she became the youngest player ever to win a match, continuing that feat through to the fourth round. By the end of the year, she was the youngest ever to be ranked in the top ten.

In 1991, Capriati became the youngest ever female semi-finalist at Wimbledon, having defeated Martina Navratilova in the quarter-finals, forcing the grand dame's earliest Wimbledon exit in 14 years. The highlight of her career came in 1992, when she beat defending champion Steffi Graf 3-6, 6-3, 6-4 to clinch the gold medal at the Barcelona Olympics.

However, it was evident that Capriati's enthusiasm for tennis was waning. Following the 1993 US Open, she stopped playing on the Tour. Soon after, she was arrested for shoplifting and spent time in a drug rehabilitation centre. After 14 months away from the Tour, she did return, but lost her first match and once again disappeared into obscurity.

On April 1, 1996, following a couple of tournaments in which she won a couple of rounds, she finally re-entered the rankings at No. 103. Since then, she has shown sparks of her old self. She beat co-No. 1 Seles en route to the 1996 Chicago final, where she lost to No. 5 Jana Novotna. Still, her ranking improved to No. 27, the highest it has been since her return to the tour. She also reached the final of the first tournament of 1997, in Sydney, where she fell to second seed Martina Hingis.

Although she continues to play, it is unlikely that Capriati will ever reach the great heights that she did in her teens. She is, it seems, a classic case of too much, too soon.

Pat Cash

STATISTICS

Date of Birth: May 27, 1965
Place of Birth: Melbourne, Australia
Place of Residence: London, England
Nationality: Australian
Height: 6ft 0in (1.83m)
Plays: Right-handed
Highest Ranking Reached: No. 4 (May 9, 1988)

Career Title Wins
Singles: 6
Doubles: 10

Grand Slam Highlights
Singles
Australian—runner-up 1987, 1988; QF 1982
Wimbledon—won 1987; SF 1984; QF 1988

Doubles
Australian—SF (w/Fitzgerald) 1984
Wimbledon—runner-up (w/McNamee) 1984, (w/Fitzgerald) 1985
US—SF (w/Fitzgerald) 1983

Pat Cash will always be remembered for clambering over Centre Court spectators when he won Wimbledon so that he could climb up the stand to embrace his girlfriend and family, and—of course—for his trademark black-and-white chequered headbands.

Other achievements of note have been few and far between, but this charismatic rock 'n' roll tennis player will always hold a special place in the hearts of spectators for his instinctive outpouring of heartfelt emotion that special day.

Cash emerged as a talent in 1982, when (at the age of 17) he won both the boys' singles titles at Wimbledon and the US Open. The following year he won his first title on the senior Tour and also reached the last 16 at Wimbledon. In 1984, he went one step further, making the semi-finals at Wimbledon and the US Open.

However, a back injury meant that he hardly played in 1985 and his ranking fell below No. 400. He made a plucky comeback in 1986, but once again his health failed. Just three weeks before Wimbledon started, he was forced to have an appendectomy. Against medical advice, he still played at the Championships thanks to a wild card and amazingly reached the quarter-finals. Later in the year, he led Australia to a thrilling Davis Cup victory over Sweden.

In 1987, Cash climbed back up the rankings, reaching the final of the Australian Open in January, followed by his famous Wimbledon win over the hapless Ivan Lendl. In 1988, he again reached the finals of the Australian Open and enjoyed considerable success on the Tour, with the result that his ranking rose to a career high when he reached No. 4 in May.

Injury, however, has continued to plague Cash since the late 1980s. A ruptured Achilles tendon, for example, sidelined him for much of 1989. Although he has made forays into the circuit since, he has not had much success at the highest levels. After the promise of his early career, it is sad that tennis watchers were only able to see him at his peak in those two winning years of 1987 and 1988.

In recent years, Cash has become better known on the tennis circuit for his guitar, rather than his racket, playing. He frequently plays at pre-Wimbledon jams and player parties; he joined John McEnroe on a record made to raise funds for the Armenian Earthquake Appeal in 1991; and he took part in a 1996 fund-raising concert for the Vitas Gerulaitis Grassroots Challenge.

Michael Chang

STATISTICS

Date of Birth: February 22, 1972
Place of Birth: Hoboken, New Jersey, USA
Place of Residence: Henderson, Nevada, USA
Nationality: US
Height: 5ft 9in (1.75m)
Plays: Right-handed
Highest Ranking Reached: No. 2 (September 9, 1996)

Career Title Wins
Singles: 31

Grand Slam Highlights
Singles
Australian—runner-up 1996; SF 1995, 1997
French—won 1989; runner-up 1995; QF 1990, 1991
US—runner-up 1996; SF 1992, 1997; QF 1993, 1995

Awards
ATP Tour Player to Watch 1988
ATP Tour Most Improved Player 1989

While Michael Chang will never be considered one of the great players of all time, he is certainly one of the most hard-working.

A streetfighter in the mould of Jimmy Connors, Chang is a tireless retriever whose ability to keep balls in play is legendary. And it is, he believes, his fighting instincts that have kept him in the higher echelons of the rankings for the last nine years.

Chang, who was introduced to tennis by his father, won his first major title, the USTA Junior Hardcourt singles, in 1984 at the age of 12. At 15, he won the USTA Boys 18s Hardcourts and the Boys 18s Nationals. As a result, he was given a wild card into the US Open, where he became the youngest player (at 15 years 6 months) to win a main draw match. A month later, he became the youngest player to reach a Tour semi-final.

In 1988, Chang captured his first Tour title and, the following year, became the youngest French Open and Grand Slam champion at 17 years, 3 months. Although he scored a thrilling five-set win over Stefan Edberg to take the title, it was his fourth round win that most fans remember over world No. 1 and French winner for the previous two years (1986, 1987) Ivan Lendl. Suffering from debilitating cramp late in a dramatically long match, which lasted 4 hours and 37 minutes, Chang actually had to serve underarm—much to the annoyance of his opponent—and yet still he beat the Czech.

Following his French Open victory, Chang climbed to No. 6 in the rankings and, three months later, to No. 5, making him the youngest player ever to make the top five. From 1990 to 1995, Chang was consistent, notching up numerous Tour wins, but his only match of note was a semi-final marathon in the 1992 US Open, when he lost to Edberg in 5hrs 26min—the longest match in Flushing Meadows' open history.

In 1995, Chang secured his strongest Grand Slam finish for six years when he reached the French Open final, falling to Thomas Muster. 1996 was better still. The Chinese American started the year by reaching his first Australian Open final, where he lost to Becker, and ended the year by advancing to his first US Open final, where he succumbed to Pete Sampras. However, he jumped to a career-high No. 2 ranking after Flushing Meadows—a win would have put him at No. 1.

Consistent results kept Chang in the world's top three players throughout 1997, a remarkable achievement for someone so often labelled only 'hard-working'.

Jimmy Connors

STATISTICS

Date of Birth: September 2, 1952
Place of Birth: Belleville, Illinois, USA
Place of Residence: Belleville, Illinois and Santa Ynez, California, USA
Nationality: US
Height: 5ft 10in (1.77m)
Plays: Left-handed
Highest Ranking Reached: No. 1 (July 29, 1974)

Career Title Wins
Singles: 109
Doubles: 19

Grand Slam Highlights
Singles
Australian—won 1974; runner-up 1975

Wimbledon—won 1974, 1982; runner-up 1975, 1977, 1978, 1984; SF 1979, 1980, 1981, 1985, 1987
US—won 1974, 1976, 1978, 1982, 1983; runner-up 1975, 1977; SF 1979, 1980, 1981, 1984, 1985, 1987, 1991; QF 1973, 1988, 1989

Doubles
French—runner-up (w/Nastase) 1973
Wimbledon—won (w/Nastase) 1973
US—won (w/Nastase) 1975

Awards
ATP Tour Player of the Year 1982
ATP Tour Comeback Player of the Year 1991

Motivation and longevity set Jimmy Connors apart from the crowd. How many other players in the modern era have competed at the highest levels on the ATP Tour at the age of 40?

Connors was playing tennis at two, encouraged by his mother, Gloria, a tennis coach. As a kid, he was smaller than his contemporaries, but he gained in grit and determination what he lost in size, and developed a solid, all-court game. His preference, however, was to slug it out from the baseline, using his double-handed backhand to great effect.

In 1972, Connors turned professional and, the same year, won his first title. Two years later, he stormed the circuit, winning the Australian Open, Wimbledon and the US Open. By July, he had been crowned No. 1, a ranking he would retain for the next 159 weeks—a record in men's tennis history.

Until 1986, Connors was never out of the top three. He won the US Open on three surfaces: on grass and clay at Forest Hills, in 1974 and 1976 respectively, and at Flushing Meadow in 1978, 1982 and 1983. He played more events, a total of 390, than any other male in history; and won more matches (1,331) and more tournaments (109) than any

other player—his last title coming in Israel in 1989.

His impact on the sport was dramatic; his popularity is credited with creating a tennis boom in the US in the late 1970s/early 1980s. Although there were times when he would behave badly on court, and irritate sponsors by ignoring protocol (as when he failed to show up for Wimbledon's Centenary Parade of Champions in 1977), fans worldwide found his never-say-die attitude, his determination and his ability to bounce back endearing.

These characteristics were never so obvious as in his penultimate year on the Tour. Surgery in 1990 meant that his ranking had dropped to No. 936, but he was determined to come back. Despite his age (38 going on 39), he played 14 tournaments in 1991 reaching Wimbledon's third round. At the US Open, he—miraculously—beat the 10th seed and four other solid players, thus reaching the semi-finals, where he fell to Jim Courier.

It would have been a fitting finale to a great career, had Connors quit tennis then. Instead he joined his contemporaries on the ATP Senior Tour and, surprise, surprise, still wins events regularly.

Jim Courier

STATISTICS

Date of Birth: August 17, 1970
Place of Birth: Sanford, Florida, USA
Place of Residence: Miami, Florida, USA
Nationality: US
Height: 6ft 1in (1.85m)
Plays: Right-handed
Highest Ranking Reached: No. 1
(February 10, 1992)

Career Title Wins
Singles: 22
Doubles: 5

Grand Slam Highlights
Singles
Australian—won 1992, 1993; SF 1994;
QF 1995, 1996
French—won 1991, 1992; runner-up
1993; SF 1994; QF 1996
Wimbledon—runner-up 1993; QF 1991
US—runner-up 1991; SF 1992, 1995

Awards
ATP Tour Most Improved Player 1991
ATP Tour Player of the Year 1992

Jim Courier is one of many successful players to have emerged from Nick Bollettieri's Tennis Academy.

During his junior career, he won the Orange Bowl in 1986 and 1987, as well as the French Open doubles title (with countryman Jonathan Stark) in 1987. He also reached the final of the USTA Boys 18s in 1987, losing to Michael Chang.

Victory at the Vina del Mar Challenger in 1988 convinced Courier that he had what was needed and that he should turn professional. It proved to be a wise decision. With his ferocious ground strokes and good all-round game, he reached two Tour semi-finals and rose fast through the rankings, ending the year at No. 43. In 1989, he grabbed his first Tour title in Basle, beating Swedish star Stefan Edberg in the final.

He wanted to become one of the top players on the Tour and he needed to win a major. In 1991 he did just that. That year turned out to be Courier's breakthrough year. He won three titles, including the Lipton (sometimes referred to as the fifth Grand Slam) and the French Open, and reached the final of the US Open and the quarter-finals of Wimbledon. As a result, his ranking rose to No. 2, within spitting distance of the top.

In February 1992, having won the Australian Open, Courier became the tenth player to be ranked No. 1 on the ATP Tour. Wins followed in Tokyo, Hong Kong, Rome and Paris, where he successfully defended his French Open title. 1993 was another good year, with Courier clinching another five Tour titles, including the Australian Open.

Since then, however, Courier's results have been erratic. Perhaps things had come too easily; perhaps there were outside attractions. Certainly in 1994 he seemed to lose interest in the Tour—he even took to reading a book in between changeovers on court!—and dropped out of the top ten. He climbed back up the rankings in 1995, but an injury to his right knee forced him off the Tour for a couple of months in 1996 and he finished out of the top 25 for the first time since turning professional in 1989.

Highlights in 1997 included his 20th Tour title and a first round drubbing of No. 1 Pete Sampras at the Italian Open, but the lowlights were four consecutive first round losses. However, in September, Courier once again started working with Brad Stine, who coached him to success in the early 1990s, so perhaps the coming years will see a revitalised Courier on Tour.

Margaret (Smith) Court

STATISTICS

Date of Birth: July 16, 1942
Place of Birth: Albury, NSW, Australia
Place of Residence: Perth, Australia
Nationality: Australian
Height: 5ft 10in (1.78m)
Plays: Right-handed
Highest Ranking Reached: No. 1 (1962)

Career Title Wins
Singles: 79
Doubles: 37

Grand Slam Highlights (only wins shown)
Singles
Australian—won 1960-66, 1969-71, 1973
French—won 1962, 1964, 1969-70, 1973
Wimbledon—won 1963, 1965, 1970
US—won 1962, 1965, 1969-70, 1973
Doubles
Australian—won (w/Reitano) 1961, (w/Ebbern) 1962-63, (w/Turner) 1965, (w/Tegart) 1969, (w/Dalton) 1970, (w/Goolagong) 1971, (w/Wade) 1973
French—won (w/Turner) 1964-65, (w/Tegart) 1966, (w/Wade) 1973
Wimbledon—won (w/Turner) 1964, (w/Tegart) 1969
US—won (w/Ebbern) 1963, (w/Bueno) 1968, (w/Dalton) 1970, (w/Wade) 1973, 1975
Mixed Doubles
Australian—won (w/Fletcher) 1963-64
French—won (w/Fletcher) 1963-65, (w/Riessen) 1969
Wimbledon—won (w/Fletcher) 1963, 1965-66, 1968, (w/Riessen) 1975
US—won (w/Mark) 1961, (w/Stolle) 1962, 1965, (w/Fletcher) 1963, (w/Newcombe) 1964, (w/Riessen) 1969, 1972, (w/Ralston) 1970

The great Margaret Smith arrived on the tennis scene in 1960, when she won her first (of 11) Australian Open singles titles. In total, she was to win an incredible 62 Grand Slam titles, the only player ever to win every major title in singles, doubles and mixed doubles.

In a 16-year career, Smith became only the second woman (the first was Maureen Connolly) to win a Grand Slam—all four majors (Australian, French, Wimbledon, US) in a calendar year. She remains the only person to have ever gained a Grand Slam in doubles (with Ken Fletcher in 1963) as well.

Her strength lay in the fact that she was equally good on all surfaces. Tall, athletic, fit and strong, Smith based her game on a hugely powerful serve and net game, managing to find incredible reach on her volleys.

However, by the end of 1966, having won all the major titles—and having lost her No. 1 ranking to Billie Jean Moffitt—Smith retired. She returned to Australia and married businessman Barry Court.

Eventually, the lure of tennis was too great and she returned to the Tour. In 1969, she won all the majors except Wimbledon. From the 1969 US Open to the French in 1971, she did not suffer another major defeat enabling her to win her Grand Slam.

Her greatest win was against Billie Jean Moffitt in the 1970 Wimbledon final. Although she had sprained her ankle, Smith rushed the net at every opportunity in order to finish the match off as quickly as possible. She won 14-12, 11-9 (in the days before the tie-break was introduced). She lost the Wimbledon 1971 final to Evonne Goolagong and then announced that she was pregnant. Her first child was born in February 1972, but, by the summer, she was back on Tour.

In 1974, Smith took a break to have her second child and the next year announced her retirement so that she could expand her family. A miscarriage in 1976 put an end to that plan and she returned to the Tour in 1977, only to discover that, again, she was expecting.

Smith's playing career was over, but she still helps to develop junior tennis talent in Australia and has a new role in life, as an ordained Minister of the church.

Lindsay Davenport

STATISTICS

Date of Birth: June 8, 1976
Place of Birth: Palos Verdes, California, USA
Place of Residence: Newport Beach, California, USA
Nationality: US
Height: 6ft 2.5in (1.89 m)
Plays: Right-handed
Highest Ranking Reached: No. 2 (November 17, 1997)

Career Title Wins
Singles: 13
Doubles: 18

Grand Slam Highlights
Singles
Australian—QF 1994, 1995
French—QF 1996
Wimbledon—QF 1994
United States—SF 1997
Doubles
Australian—runner-up (w/Fernandez) 1996, (w/Raymond) 1997
French—won (w/Fernandez) 1996; runner-up (w/Raymond) 1994
US—won (w/Novotna) 1997
Mixed Doubles
Australian—SF (w/Connell) 1995
Wimbledon—SF (w/Connell) 1995, 1996, 1997

Lindsay Davenport comes from a sporting family—her mother is president of the Southern California Volleyball Association, both her sisters played college volleyball and her father participated in the 1968 Olympics.

Davenport started playing tennis at the age of seven and soon rose through the ranks of junior competition. In 1992, she won the US Open girls' singles and doubles, as well as the Australian Open junior doubles (both with Nicole London). A week after turning professional, in February 1993, Davenport upset the world's then No. 5 ranked player, Gabriela Sabatini. A few months later, she won her first major tour event, the 1993 European Open, and her ranking jumped to No. 25.

Following consistent results, such as a quarter-final finish at the Australian Open, Davenport entered the top ten in May 1994. She also graduated from her High School.

Concentrating on the Tour in 1995, Davenport notched up some impressive results. In the Grand Slams, she reached the singles' quarter-finals, doubles semi-finals and mixed doubles semi-final of the Australian Open, and the semi-finals of the French Open doubles and the mixed doubles at Wimbledon. She also won three Tour events.

1996 was a particularly good year. She triumphed at the French Open with a career best quarter-final place in the singles and won the doubles (her first Grand Slam title) with compatriot Mary Jo Fernandez. In August, she beat world co-No. 1 Steffi Graf en route to the Los Angeles title, becoming the first player to defeat the German in straight sets in almost two years. A few weeks later, Davenport entered the top five in the world. She also won a gold medal at the Atlanta Olympics.

Proving that she is a force to be reckoned with, Davenport was victorious over the No. 1-ranked Martina Hingis in the semi-finals of the 1997 Los Angeles event. It was only the second loss of the year for the Swiss youngster, and meant that Davenport could now claim to be the only player to have beaten both Hingis and Graf when they were No. 1.

A strong finish to the year saw the American reach her first Grand Slam semi-final, at the US Open, and clinch the doubles crown with Czech Jana Novotna. By the end of the year, Davenport had registered career-high world rankings in singles (No. 2) and doubles (No. 1), giving an indication of the power house that she is likely to be for some years to come.

Stefan Edberg

STATISTICS

Date of Birth: January 19, 1966
Place of Birth: Vastervik, Sweden
Place of Residence: London, England
Nationality: Swedish
Height: 6ft 2in (1.88m)
Plays: Right-handed
Highest Ranking Reached: No. 1 (August 13, 1990)

Career Title Wins
Singles: 41
Doubles: 18

Grand Slam Highlights
Singles
Australian—won 1985, 1987; runner-up 1990, 1992, 1993; SF 1988, 1991, 1994; QF 1984, 1989

French—runner-up 1989; QF 1985, 1991, 1993
Wimbledon—won 1988, 1990; runner-up 1989; SF 1987, 1991, 1993; QF 1992
US—won 1991, 1992; SF 1986, 1987; QF 1996

Doubles
Australian—won (w/Jarryd) 1987, (w/Korda) 1996
French—runner-up (w/Jarryd) 1986
US—won (w/Jarryd) 1987; runner-up (w/Jarryd) 1984

Awards
ATP Tour Player of the Year 1990, 1991
ATP Tour Doubles Team of the Year (w/Jarryd) 1987
ATP Tour Sportsmanship Award 1988, 1989, 1990, 1992, 1995

Stefan Edberg is a great champion in the league of Andre Agassi, Boris Becker and John McEnroe, but will he be remembered as such? Probably not—and for all the right reasons: he never demonstrated the flamboyance of Agassi, the brute force of Becker or the abuse of McEnroe. He was, instead, a true gentleman, a graceful serve and volleyer, who won the ATP Tour Sportsmanship Award so many times that in 1996 it was named after him.

He began playing tennis at the age of seven, but only decided to dedicate himself to the sport at 16, when he was European Junior Champion for the second time. A year later, Edberg captured a junior Grand Slam and was the No. 1 ranked junior in the world.

Turning professional, he made an impression on the Tour immediately. He won a Tour title in his first year, as well as the gold medal at the 1984 Los Angeles Olympics, where tennis was a demonstration sport. By the end of 1985, having won the Australian Open to claim his first major at senior level, he had already broken into the top five.

Unlike many of his fellow Swedes, who preferred to play on clay, it was on fast sur-faces that Edberg was to achieve his greatest success. He won the Australian Open again in 1987 (the last year it was on grass), Wimbledon in 1989 and 1990. He then won the US Open on the hard courts of Flushing Meadow in 1991 and 1992.

Fast courts suited Edberg's attacking style of play much better. His serve and volley repertoire consisted of a hammering serve, as well as a difficult kicker, a wicked backhand and some of the finest volleys of modern times. He could play on clay too, as he proved by reaching the French Open final in 1989.

In 1990, having been runner-up at the Australian Open and champion of Wimbledon, followed by three consecutive Tour titles, Edberg finally reached No. 1. He would remain in the top ten until the end of 1994, joining the elite (Jimmy Connors, Ivan Lendl and McEnroe) who have stayed in the top ten for ten years running.

Edberg was also a proficient doubles player—he reached five Grand Slam finals with two different partners, winning three titles.

Chris Evert (Mills)

STATISTICS

Date of Birth: December 21, 1954
Place of Birth: Fort Lauderdale, Florida, USA
Places of Residence: Boca Raton, Florida
and Aspen, Colorado, USA
Nationality: US
Height: 5ft 6in (1.68m)
Plays: Right-handed
Highest Ranking Reached: No. 1
(November 1975)

Career Title Wins
Singles: 157
Doubles: 8

Grand Slam Highlights (wins only shown)
Singles
Australian—won 1982, 1984

French—won 1974, 1975, 1979, 1980,
1983, 1985, 1986
Wimbledon—won 1974, 1976, 1981
US—won 1975, 1976, 1977, 1978, 1980,
1982

Doubles
French—won (w/Morozova) 1974,
(w/Navratilova) 1975
Wimbledon—won (w/Navratilova) 1976

Awards
WTA Tour Player of the Year 1981
WTA Tour Player Service Award 1985, 1987
WTA Tour Sportsmanship Award 1979
WTA Tour Special Service Award 1992
WTA Tour Honorary Membership Award 1992

Chris Evert changed the face of tennis by inspiring a generation of baseliners with two-handed backhands. Although it was a style of play that many found boring, she used it intelligently, producing flawless barrages to manoeuvre opponents into a position that would allow her to make a winning shot.

She started playing at five, taught by her father Jimmy, who won the Canadian singles title in 1947. She was just 15 when she beat the reigning Grand Slam champion and world No. 1, Margaret Smith, in September 1970.

The following year, while still a schoolgirl, she reached the semi-finals of the US Open. In 1972, Evert made the semi-finals of both Wimbledon and the US Open, but it was not until December 21 (the day of her 18th birthday) that she turned professional. Her progression was swift.

In 1973, she reached the finals of the French Open and Wimbledon. In 1974, the titles started to flood in. Evert won her first Grand Slam, the French Open, and then took Wimbledon. A year later, having won the French and US Opens, she reached No. 1—a ranking she was to retain until 1978.

The 1980s marked the start of one of the greatest rivalries in the history of tennis. More contrasting characters than Evert and Martina Navratilova do not exist. Evert was the feminine, pretty all-American girl to Navratilova's Eastern bloc athleticism; the Ice Queen to the girl who wore her emotions on her sleeve; the baseliner to the serve and volleyer. For four years (1982-85), these two players shared all the Grand Slam titles but one (the 1985 US Open won by Hana Mandlikova).

In the late 1980s, Evert entered the twilight of her career, but by then she had already racked up some amazing records. For example, she reached the semi-finals or better at 52 of her last 56 Grand Slams; won at least one Grand Slam per year for 13 years (1974-86); was never ranked lower than No. 4 for 18 years (1972-89); has the best record on clay (on which she was raised) of any player on any single surface—a 125-match, 24-tournament winning streak from August 1973 to May 1979; owns the highest winning percentage in professional tennis (90%); was the first player, male or female, to win 1,000 matches.

These days she is married to Andy Mills (an ex-Olympic downhill skier) and is the mother of three boys.

Vitus Gerulaitis

STATISTICS

Date of Birth: July 26, 1954
Place of Birth: Brooklyn, New York, USA
Date of Death: September 17, 1994
Nationality: US
Height: 5ft 10in (1.78m)
Played: Right-handed
Highest Ranking Reached: No. 3 (February 27, 1978)

Career Title Wins
Singles: 27
Doubles: 9

Grand Slam Highlights
Singles
Australian—won 1977
French—runner-up 1980; SF 1979; QF 1982
Wimbledon—SF 1977, 1978; QF 1976, 1982
US—runner-up 1979; SF 1978, 1981

Doubles
Wimbledon—won (w/Mayer) 1975

Awards
ATP Tour Most Improved Player 1975
ATP Tour Player to Watch 1975

It was almost inevitable that Vitas Gerulaitis would become a tennis player. His father, also Vitas, was the tennis champion of his native Lithuania and, in the United States, where the children grew up, there were even greater opportunities to play the game.

Unfortunately, despite being a great tennis talent, Gerulaitis never really fulfilled the promise that he displayed early on in his career when he was voted the ATP Tour's Most Improved Player *and* Player to Watch in 1975. Likewise, his sister, Ruta, who played on the women's Tour, did not achieve huge success—she peaked at No. 31 in November 1980.

Unfortunately, Gerulaitis, who had a strong, all-round game which he sometimes used to produce electrifying tennis, also went through terrible periods of uncertainty and loss of motivation. Perhaps his greatest 'disadvantage' was his zest for life. He had an insatiable appetite for fun and parties that was impossible to match. Easygoing, with a heart of gold, he was always upbeat and had a smile on his face. As one of his contemporaries once said, 'When Vitas is around, anything can happen.'

Events that Gerulaitis could have done without included a drugs incident, suspension for bad behaviour not once, but twice, in 1981 and a loss to Martina Navratilova and Pam Shriver, when he and Bobby Riggs took them on in a 'Battle of the Sexes' doubles match in 1985.

However, there were good times, too. Guided by the Australian champion Fred Stolle, Gerulaitis, who was a speedy, lean and determined attacker, won his one and only Grand Slam singles title, the Australian Open in 1977, and the Italian Open twice (1977 and 1979). He also reached the final of the French Open in 1980 (where he lost to Bjorn Borg) and of the US Open in 1979, when he lost to John McEnroe.

However, the match for which he will probably best be remembered is his 1977 Wimbledon semi-final match against great friend and regular practice partner, Bjorn Borg. The fact that the two knew each other's game so well produced a classic encounter, the outcome of which was in doubt right up until the last ball was struck, but it was the Swede who won the electrifying five set match.

Vitas Gerulaitis's sparkling life was cut tragically short soon after his 40th birthday, when he was gassed by a faulty domestic heating system.

Evonne Goolagong (Cawley)

STATISTICS

Date of Birth: July 31, 1951
Place of Birth: Griffith, New South Wales, Australia
Place of Residence: Australia
Nationality: Australian
Height: 5ft 6in (1.68m)
Plays: Right-handed
Highest Ranking Reached: No.2 (April 1976)

Career Title Wins
Singles: 88
Doubles: 11

Grand Slam Highlights
Singles
Australian—won 1974, 1975, 1976, 1977; runner-up 1971, 1972, 1973; QF 1981

French—won 1971; runner-up 1972; SF 1973
Wimbledon—won 1971, 1980; runner-up 1972, 1975, 1976; SF 1973, 1978, 1979; QF 1974
US—runner-up 1973, 1974, 1975, 1976; QF 1979

Doubles
Australian—won 1971 (w/Court), 1974 (w/Michel), 1975 (w/Michel), 1976 (w/Gourlay)
Wimbledon—won 1974 (w/Michel); runner-up 1971 (w/Court)

Awards
WTA Tour Sportsmanship Award 1980

Of all the champions that have emerged from Australia, the most improbable is Evonne Goolagong—the only person of Aboriginal extraction to have became an international tennis player.

One of eight children born to a sheep shearer, she grew up in the country west of Sydney. Peering through the fence at the local tennis courts one day, a kindly resident invited Goolagong to play. It turned out that she was a natural: she had speed, lightning reflexes and a perfect temperament in equal measure. Although she never hit the ball hard, she could find the most acute angles and was a good volleyer, which made her particularly effective on grass.

At the age of 13, in order to develop her tennis further, Goolagong moved to Sydney to live with Vic Edwards, one of the country's top coaches. Under his tutelage, in 1971 (only her second year on the Tour and before she had turned 20), Goolagong won the French Open defeating Helen Gourlay (another Australian) and Wimbledon, crushing her compatriot and childhood idol, Margaret Smith, in a straight sets final, 6-4, 6-1.

Goolagong captivated the crowds wherever she went and was dubbed the 'Sunshine Supergirl' by the British tabloids because of her graceful manner and breezy nature. Whether she was winning or losing, she always seemed to be in a good mood.

Her performance throughout the remainder of the 1970s can best be described as mediocre. Although she won the Australian Open four times, beating Chris Evert and Martina Navratilova in 1974 and 1975 respectively, she did not win any of the overseas majors.

In 1975, Evonne Goolagong married an Englishman, Roger Cawley, and missed the 1977 season to have her first child. On her return, she scored a unique success: she won Wimbledon for a second time, after a nine-year gap and having had her first baby. She was the first mother to win the title since Dorothea Lambert Chambers 66 years earlier. She beat Chris Evert 6-1, 7-6.

Goolagong missed the 1981 season to have her second child and on her return, in 1982, was humiliated by the young American Zina Garrison. She retired at the end of the 1983 season, but still competes in special events.

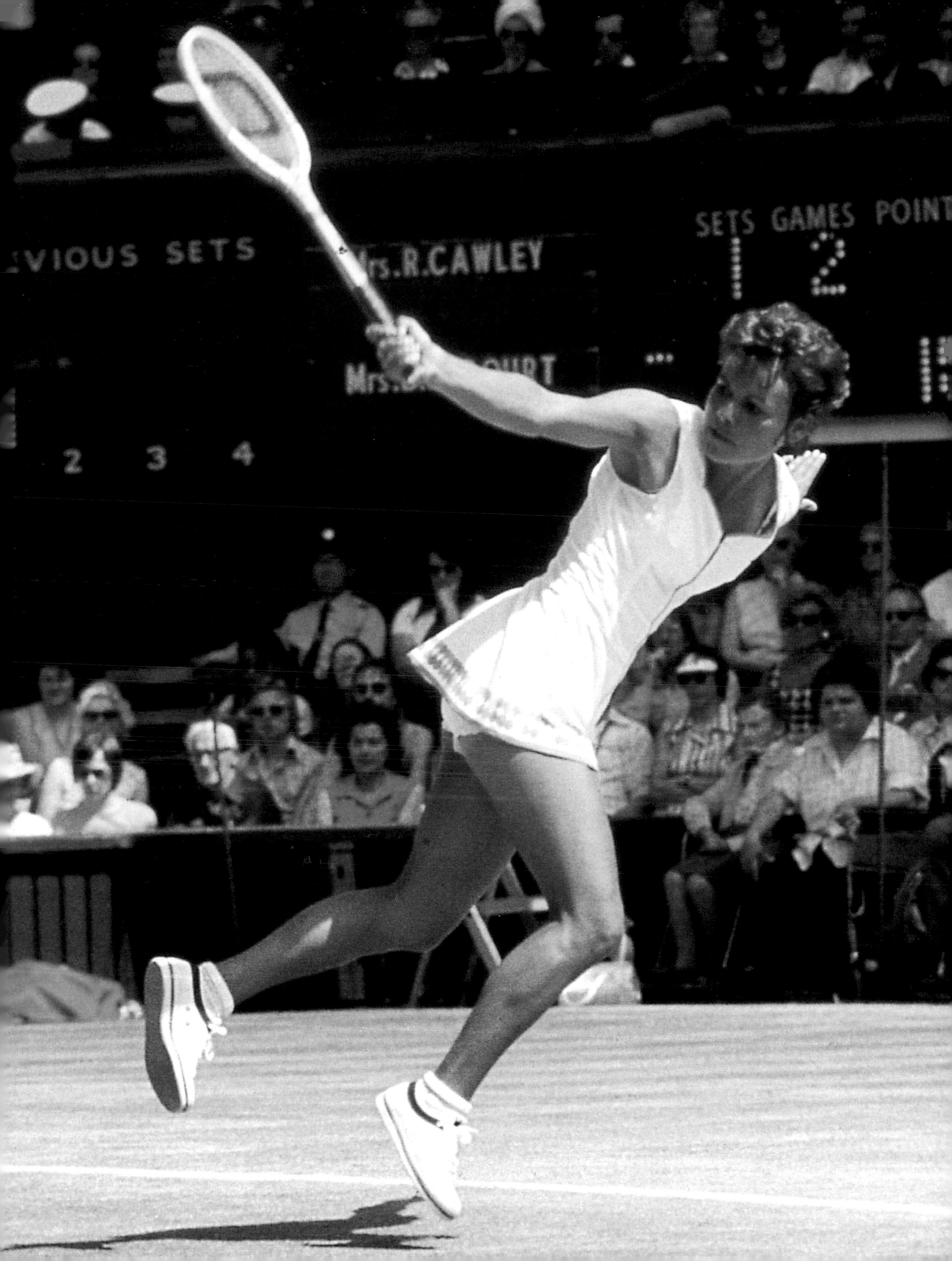
SETS GAMES POINT
EVIOUS SETS
rs.R.CAWLEY
1 2
2 3 4

Steffi Graf

STATISTICS

Date of Birth: June 14, 1969
Place of Birth: Bruhl, Germany
Place of Residence: Bruhl, Germany
Nationality: German
Height: 5ft 9in (1.75 m)
Plays: Right-handed
Highest Ranking Reached: No. 1 (August 17, 1987)

Career Title Wins
Singles: 103
Doubles: 11

Grand Slam Highlights wins only shown
Singles
Australian—won 1988-90, 1994
French—won 1987-88, 1993, 1995-96
Wimbledon—won 1988-89, 1991-93, 1995-96
US—won 1988-89, 1993, 1995-96

Doubles
Wimbledon—won (w/Sabatini) 1988

Awards
WTA Tour Player of the Year 1987, 1988, 1989, 1990, 1993, 1994, 1995, 1996
WTA Tour Most Improved Player 1986

If Steffi Graf is remembered for one thing, it will be her 1988 Golden Grand Slam. Only the fifth player to win a Grand Slam, she made hers unique by also winning a gold medal at the Olympics.

Graf started playing tennis at four, when she persuaded her father to set up a 'court' in the family living room. At 11, she won the Orange Bowl and, at 12, the 1982 European Championships 12s and 18s. At 13 years 4 months, she became the youngest player ever to turn professional.

In her first couple of years on Tour, Graf's only win of note was the 1984 Olympics. In 1986, however, she challenged the stranglehold at the very top of the rankings, scoring her first wins over Chris Evert and Martina Navratilova, and her ranking jumped to No. 3. With her powerful forehand, she soon became known to the Press as 'Fraulein Forehand'.

1987 marked a turning point for Graf. Days before her 18th birthday, she won her first Grand Slam title, the French Open, and in August she snatched the No. 1 ranking from Martina Navratilova. It was a position she was to retain for a record 186 weeks.

1988 was a hard year to follow, but Graf came close. She won all the Grand Slam events, except the French, and finished the year with a near perfect 86-2 (97.7 per cent) win-loss record.

Although Graf won the Australian Open in 1990, her play suffered in the rest of the year, as her beloved father was embroiled in a scandal. In March 1991, Graf's domination of the women's game ended when Monica Seles bulldozed her way to the top of the rankings. Between them, they captured all the major titles in 1991 and 1992, with Graf winning at Wimbledon both years. Their rivalry would undoubtedly have continued to fascinate the public if a deranged Graf fan had not stabbed Seles in the back in April 1993.

With Seles in rehabilitation, Graf once again took control of the Tour, winning the next four Grand Slam titles to become the only woman other than Navratilova to have won a non-calendar Grand Slam.

In recent years, Graf's personal problems have overshadowed her tennis. Although she won all six Grand Slams she entered in 1995 and 1996, allegations of tax fraud against her father and, indirectly, herself were clearly preying on her mind. Injuries, which have plagued her career, have also taken their toll. In December 1995, she underwent surgery on her left foot, followed 18 months later by an operation to repair her left knee.

In March 1997, having held the No. 1 spot for a total of 374 non-consecutive weeks, Graf was nudged off the top ranking spot by Martina Hingis.

Tim Henman

STATISTICS

Date of Birth: September 6, 1974
Place of Birth: Oxford, England
Place of Residence: London, England
Nationality: British
Height: 6ft 1in (1.85m)
Plays: Right-handed
Highest Ranking Reached: No. 14
(January 13, 1997)

Career Title Wins
Singles: 2
Doubles: 1

Grand Slam Highlights
Wimbledon—QF 1996, 1997

Awards
ATP Tour Most Improved Player 1996

In 1995, Tim Henman only made the news because he became the first person ever to be disqualified from Wimbledon. A year later, it was a different story. By reaching the quarter-finals of Wimbledon, the first Brit to do so since Roger Taylor in 1973, he became an overnight hero.

Henman comes from a long line of tennis players. His great grandmother, Ellen Stowell-Brown, was the first woman to serve overarm at Wimbledon and two grandparents, Henry and Susan Billington, played there, too, his grandfather reaching the third round.

Henman started playing with his parents, both of county standard, at the age of three. By the age of five or six, so he claims, he knew he wanted to be a professional tennis player. At 11, he won a tennis scholarship to Reeds School, Surrey and in 1992 captured the national 18-under singles title.

A year later, Henman started on the professional Tour, making his way up the rankings by playing in Satellites and Challengers, the two tiers below main Tour events. In 1994, he qualified for his first Tour event, but soon afterwards broke his leg in three places in a freak, on-court incident.

Henman returned with a vengeance in 1995, winning two Challengers, reaching his first Tour quarter-finals at Nottingham and the second round at Wimbledon, where he lost to Pete Sampras. By playing the world's best, on his favourite surface, Henman realised just how much he had to do to improve his game.

Putting what he had learnt into practice, the Brit advanced to six semi-finals and, most importantly, the quarter-finals at Wimbledon in 1996. The nation was swept by 'Henmania'—thousands of fans watched his every move and a police guard accompanied him everywhere. All the supporters in the world, however, could not have stopped Henman being beaten by the American Todd Martin in the round of eight.

After Wimbledon, Henman made his first top 50 appearance, rising from No. 62 to No. 39. Surprisingly, as he has never had a high doubles ranking, he then went to the Atlanta Olympics and won a silver medal with Neil Broad.

1997 started well for Henman. He won his first Tour event in Sydney, defeating Goran Ivanisevic of Croatia in the semi-finals and Spain's Carlos Moya for the title. He subsequently broke into the top 20, recording a career best No. 14. However, he had to miss nearly two months from March to May in order to undergo surgery on his right elbow.

At Wimbledon, Henman brushed aside defending champion Richard Krajicek and Paul Haarhuis on his way to a repeat quarter-final finish, where he lost to Michael Stich. In September, he won his second Tour title in Tashkent. In total, Henman was ranked in the top 20 for all but six weeks of 1997.

Martina Hingis

STATISTICS

Date of Birth: September 30, 1980
Place of Birth: Kosice, Slovakia
Place of Residence: Trubbach, Switzerland
Nationality: Swiss
Height: 5ft 6in (1.67m)
Plays: Right-handed
Highest Ranking Reached: No. 1 (March 31, 1997)

Career Title Wins
Singles: 13
Doubles: 11

Grand Slam Highlights
Singles
Australian—won 1997; QF 1996
French—runner-up 1997
Wimbledon—won 1997
US—won 1997; SF 1996

Doubles
Australian—won (w/Zvereva) 1997
French—SF (w/Sanchez Vicario) 1997; QF (w/Sukova) 1997
Wimbledon—won (w/Sukova) 1996; QF (w/Sanchez Vicario) 1997
US—SF (w/Sukova) 1996, (w/Sanchez Vicario) 1997

Doubles, Mixed
French—QF (w/de Jager) 1996
Wimbledon—QF (w/Philippoussis) 1997
US—SF (w/van Rensburg) 1996

Awards
WTA Tour Most Improved Player 1996
WTA Tour Most Impressive Newcomer Award 1995

Some might think the pressure of being named one of the best female tennis players ever, would be too much of a burden to bear, but it does not appear to have affected the Martina Hingis, who was trained from the age of three by her mother, Melanie Molitor, to follow in her namesake Martina Navratilova's footsteps.

Following a very successful junior career, Hingis made her professional debut on the WTA Tour and steadily made her way up the world rankings. Always happy, with a ready smile on her lips, she enjoys ordinary teenage pursuits such as inline skating, horse-riding and cycling, while displaying extraordinary skill on the tennis court.

She has been compared with Evonne Cawley because of her fluidity on court and blithe, carefree spirit; with Chris Evert-Mills for her precocious poise, pinpoint accurate ground strokes and economy of game; and with Tracy Austin because of her explosive double-handed backhand down the line.

Although still young, her achievements already speak for themselves. She is:

- the youngest ever Wimbledon champion as a result of the 1996 ladies' doubles title won with the Czech Helena Sukova
- at 16 years 1 month 10 days, the youngest tennis player ever, male or female, to earn US$1 million in prize money
- the youngest player (aged 16 years 3 months 26 days when she won the 1997 Australian Open) in the 20th century to win a Grand Slam singles title
- the youngest No. 1-ranked player, at 16 years 6 months 1 day (on March 31, 1997), since computer rankings began in 1975
- the youngest player in the Open era (since 1968) to have won a singles title at Wimbledon, which she won in 1997 aged 16 years 9 months 5 days

And so the list goes on, and, will no doubt continue to grow, as this young star looks ahead to a glorious future.

Yevgeny Kafelnikov

STATISTICS

Date of Birth: February 18, 1974
Place of Birth: Sochi, Russia
Place of Residence: Sochi, Russia
Nationality: Russian
Height: 6ft 3in (1.90m)
Plays: Right-handed
Highest Ranking Reached: No. 3
(November 4, 1996)

Career Title Wins
Singles: 14
Doubles: 16

Grand Slam Highlights
Singles
Australian—QF 1995, 1996
French—won 1996; SF 1995; QF 1997
Wimbledon—QF 1995

Doubles
French—won (w/Vacek) 1996, 1997
Wimbledon—SF (w/Goellner) 1994, 1995
US—won (w/Vacek) 1997

Awards
ATP Tour Most Improved Player 1994

Yevgeny Kafelnikov has a mixed sporting lineage—his father is a high school volleyball coach, while his mother played college basketball. Kafelnikov began playing tennis at the age of six. It was a match win at the 1992 Tour event in Moscow that set him on the professional path.

Almost immediately, he started producing amazing results in both singles and doubles. In 1993, Kafelnikov beat Michael Stich, then a top ten player, twice, and won a single and doubles title (with Dutchman Hendrik Jan Davids) at Challenger level. In 1994, following two singles titles and four doubles titles, he finished No. 11 in singles and No. 12 in doubles.

In 1995, Kafelnikov continued to show his versatility by playing 167 matches (the most on the Tour), and being the only player to win four singles (on three different surfaces) and four doubles titles. A quarter-final finish at the Australian Open took his ranking into the top ten, where he remained for the rest of the year. By year end, his doubles ranking was also in the top ten.

1996 was a breakthrough year for the young Russian. Having reached the semi-finals of the French Open the previous year by beating then-No. 1 Andre Agassi, Kafelnikov went two better and won at Roland Garros. It was his first Grand Slam title and the first ever for a Russian. His success did not surprise many—No. 1 Pete Sampras had already picked out Kafelnikov as a great player.

In claiming the doubles title (with Czech Daniel Vacek), Kafelnikov became the first player since Ken Rosewall in 1968 to win both French titles. At the end of the year, he was the first player since John McEnroe in 1989 to finish in the top five in singles (No. 3) and doubles (No. 5).

Unfortunately, 1997 started badly for Kafelnikov when he fractured a finger and was away from the Tour for three months. On his return, however, he reached the quarter-finals of the French Open (losing to eventual winner Gustavo Kuerten) and the following week proved he could win on grass by beating Stich, Boris Becker and Petr Korda to win at Halle.

In total, Kafelnikov won three events in 1997, plus three doubles titles (including two Grand Slams). Once again, he ended the year in both the singles and doubles top ten.

Billie Jean (Moffitt) King

STATISTICS

Date of Birth: November 22, 1943
Place of Birth: Long Beach, California, USA
Place of Residence: New York, New York State, USA
Nationality: US
Height: 5ft 4.5in (1.64m)
Plays: Right-handed
Highest Ranking Reached: No. 1 (1966)

Career Title Wins
Singles: 67
Doubles: 20

Grand Slam Highlights (only wins shown)
Singles
Australian—won 1968
French—won 1972
Wimbledon—won 1966, 1967, 1968, 1972, 1973, 1975
US—won 1967, 1971, 1972, 1974

Doubles
French—won 1972 (w/Stove)
Wimbledon—won (w/Hantze) 1961, (w/Susman) 1962, (w/Bueno) 1965, (w/Casals) 1967, 1968, 1970, 1971, 1973, (w/Stove) 1972, (w/Navratilova) 1979
US—won (w/Susman) 1964, (w/Casals) 1967, 1974, (w/Navratilova) 1978, 1980

Mixed
Australian—won (w/Crealy) 1968

Awards
WTA Tour Doubles Team of the Year (w/Navratilova) 1978, 1979
WTA Tour Special Service Award 1993
WTA Tour Honorary Membership Award 1986

Billie Jean Moffitt was not only a great player, she was also an outspoken reformer of women's tennis. She campaigned endlessly for women's equality in tennis, seeking as much coverage as the men's Tour and equal pay. To aid her cause, she set up the WTA in 1973. It is largely due to her that the women's game receives the recognition it does today.

Moffitt first hit the headlines in 1961, when she and 18-year old Karen Hantze became the youngest pair ever to win the Wimbledon doubles title. It was the start of one of the longest top class careers in the modern era, stretching up to 1983. In that time, she was to win every single title at the four majors and a record 20 Wimbledon titles.

Wimbledon was definitely a very special place for Moffitt. She reached at least the quarter-finals every time she played in the singles and played so many matches—a record 265—that the Centre Court became known as 'The Old Lady's House' (Moffitt being known as 'The Old Lady'), so much time did she spend on it.

A natural grass court player, Moffitt was quick, aggressive and liked to serve and volley, so she was at her best at Wimbledon. However, she could play on all surfaces, as she proved by winning all the Grand Slam events at least once.

She could even play, and beat, the men. In the 'Battle of the Sexes', which took place on September 20, 1973 in front of a television audience of some 90 million, she defeated Bobby Riggs, the 1939 Wimbledon men's champion, 6-4, 6-3, 6-3.

Aside from actually playing tennis, she and her husband, Larry King, established the World Team Tennis League, a professional tennis circuit in the United States involving a mixed team playing for a particular town.

In 1983, Moffitt became the oldest woman to win a professional Tour title, winning the Birmingham event at the age of 39 years and 6 months. Her final swansong came at Wimbledon 1983, when she once again reached the semi-finals, losing to her 18 year old compatriot, Andrea Jaeger.

Petr Korda

STATISTICS

Date of Birth: January 23, 1968
Place of Birth: Prague, Czechoslovakia
Place of Residence: Monte Carlo, Monaco
Nationality: Czech
Height: 6ft 3in (1.90m)
Plays: Left-handed
Highest Ranking Reached: No. 5 (July 6, 1992)

Career Title Wins
Singles: 8
Doubles: 10

Grand Slam Highlights
Singles
Australian—QF 1993
French—runner-up 1992
US—QF 1995, 1997

Doubles
Australian—won (w/Edberg) 1996; SF (w/P. McEnroe) 1995
French—runner-up (w/Ivanisevic) 1990; SF (w/Edberg) 1993

Petr Korda looked as if he was going to be yet another player who had failed to fulfil his potential, until he won the Australian Open at the start of 1998.

Korda was coached by his father until the age of 18, but as a youngster used to ball-boy for Ivan Lendl during Davis Cup matches, so he picked up tips from one of the all-time greats. By the age of 16, he was Czech Junior Champion. Two years later, he was crowned world 18s doubles champion (with Cyril Suk), even though he captured the Wimbledon junior doubles title with Spain's Tomas Carbonell.

In 1987, Korda powered his way into the top 100, winning the Budapest Challenger and reaching the quarter-finals of his Tour debut in Prague. In 1989, he took giant steps up the rankings, moving 224 spots within a three-month period. He continued to post solid results through 1990 and 1991, resulting in a top ten finish at the end of the year.

Korda's big break came in 1992, when he marched through to the final of the French Open, having never previously been past the third round in a major. Unfortunately, as happens so often, nerves got the better of him and his usual free-swinging style was curbed. As a result, he fell to Jim Courier, in straight sets, 7-5, 6-2, 6-1, explaining afterwards, 'I

think I played with big feet today. I tell you I was very nervous.'

Still, Korda continued to win Tour titles and in 1993 had played well enough during the year to qualify for the Grand Slam Cup in which he beat world No. 1 Pete Sampras. The following year, the Czech was ranked in the top 20 every week and proved he is a skilful all-rounder, reaching finals on three different surfaces: carpet, hard courts and clay.

A nagging left groin injury hampered Korda's progress during 1995 and, finally, he agreed to an operation in October. Although this meant that he finished outside the top twenty for the first time since 1990, he bounced back in 1996, winning his first Grand Slam title—the doubles with Stefan Edberg at the Australian Open—and finished the year in the top thirty in singles and doubles— all this despite the fact that he underwent a right groin operation in June.

1997 proved to be a good one for Korda. He notched up some good results on all surfaces, winning a title in Stuttgart, and returned to the top ten. 1998, however, might just be his best year yet. It certainly started well, with a straight sets win over Marcelo Rios in the final of the Australian Open. After his poor performance at the French Open in 1992, Korda ensured there were no mistakes this time.

Anna Kournikova

STATISTICS

Date of Birth: June 7, 1981
Place of Birth: Moscow, Russia
Place of Residence: Bradenton, Florida, USA
Nationality: Russian
Height: 5ft 8in (1.73 m)
Plays: Right-handed
Highest Ranking Reached: No. 25 (July 7, 1997)

Grand Slam Highlights
Singles
Wimbledon—SF 1997

Mixed Doubles
Australian—QF (w/Knowles) 1997
French—QF (w/Knowles) 1997

Awards
WTA Tour Most Impressive Newcomer 1996

Anna Kournikova is the latest glamour girl to grace the women's Tour—just what the tabloid press needed, a replacement for Gabriela Sabatini.

She began playing tennis at the age of five in a children's sports programme and, at the age of ten, was spotted by tennis guru Nick Bollettieri playing an exhibition match in Russia. He invited her to join his tennis academy—the famous academy which has produced, among others, such stars as Andre Agassi, Jim Courier and Mary Pierce—and so, in February 1992, Kournikova and her mother moved to Florida, where Bollettieri continues to train her.

Although still young, Anna Kournikova had already had a successful junior career. In 1995, while still only 14, she won the Orange Bowl 18s, the European Championships 18s and the Italian Open junior event. She also reached the semi-finals of junior Wimbledon and the quarter-finals of the French Open junior event. At the end of the year, she was named ITF Junior World Champion.

The following year, the blonde Russian became the youngest player to compete in, and win, a Federation Cup tie, helping Russia defeat Sweden 3-0.

Success on the lower ranks of the women's Tour has followed. As a qualifier, she won her first professional title at a 1996 ITF Women's Circuit satellite event in Midland, Michigan. Then, having played the final, she flew to Oklahoma City in time to win her first-round qualifying match the same day. Seeded fifth, she won her second title at a 1996 ITF Women's Circuit satellite event in Rockford, Illinois.

In 1996, Kournikova started playing on the main Tour. The spotlight was bound to be on her early because of her looks, but she responded brilliantly: in the US Open, her first Grand Slam event, she reached the fourth round, beating the 14th seed, Austria's Barbara Paulus, en route. The following month, as a wild card ranked No. 84, she defeated South Africa's Amanda Coetzer, ranked No. 13, in the first round. As a result, her ranking immediately jumped 26 spots to a then-career high No. 58.

1997 was by far the best year yet for Kournikova. She collected her first win over a top ten player, beating the sixth-ranked player—herself no pushover, the mercurial Spaniard Arantxa Sanchez Vicario—in Berlin, and her ranking jumped for the first time into the top fifty. She also became only the second woman in the open era to reach the Wimbledon semi-finals in her career debut in the tournament—she's in good company. One of the great champions, Chris Evert, is the other in 1972. On her way to the last four, she defeated the fifth-ranked Croatian Iva Majoli in the quarter-finals and the 10th-ranked Anke Huber of Germany in the third round.

With her all-court style of game, Kournikova looks set to be a feature on the women's Tour for some time to come.

Gustavo Kuerten

STATISTICS

Date of Birth: September 10, 1976
Place of Birth: Florianopolis, Brazil
Place of Residence: Florianopolis, Brazil
Nationality: Brazilian
Height: 6ft 3in (1.90m)
Plays: Right-handed
Highest Ranking Reached: No. 8 (August 11, 1997)

Career Title Wins
Singles: 1
Doubles: 4

Grand Slam Highlights
Singles
French—won 1997

Gustavo Kuerten is the flamboyant, brightly attired youngster whose dreams came true when he came from nowhere to win his first Tour title ever . . . and it just happened to be the 1997 French Open.

Kuerten, whose nickname is Guga, began playing tennis at the age of eight. He is not the only player in his family—his older brother, Rafael, is a tennis teacher in his hometown of Florianopolis.

In 1994, Kuerten was one of the top juniors in the world, with a year end ranking of No. 6 in singles and No. 4 in doubles. His best results that year were a place in the final of the Orange Bowl 18s, which he lost to fellow South American Nicolas Lapentti, and the French Open Junior doubles title, which he won with the same Lapentti.

In his first full year on the Tour, Kuerten improved his ranking more than 200 places with success at the Challenger level. He reached the final of the Medellin Challenger, losing to France's Jerome Golmard, and enjoyed semi-final and quarter-final finishes at a handful of Challengers, mostly in Latin America.

In April 1996, in Prague, he qualified for his first career ATP Tour event and won his first round match against Russian Andrei Chesnokov, marking his first ever Tour victory. Further success at Challenger level, plus two quarter-final finishes at the Tour level, resulted in him breaking into the top 100 for the first time—he finished the year ranked No. 88, making him Brazil's top player.

1997 was a fairy tale come true for Kuerten. When he won the French Open in early June, he became the first Brazilian to win a Grand Slam singles title since the balletic Maria Bueno in the 1960s and the second lowest ranked player, at No. 66, to be a Grand Slam champion. His ranking subsequently moved up to No. 15.

Proving that he is not just a flash in the pan, the 20-year old continued to play well in 1997, reaching the final in Bologna the week after his win in Paris. However, he is not just a clay court specialist. On the hard courts of Montreal in August, he again reached the final, beating Michael Chang in the semis.

At the end of the year, Kuerten had won US$1,586,753—quite a leap from the US$113,835, he had pocketed in 1996! The Brazilian also plays doubles, most often with compatriot Fernando Meligeni. They won their first ATP Tour title together in 1996, followed by a further three in 1997.

Rod Laver

STATISTICS

Date of Birth: August 9, 1938
Place of Birth: Rockhampton, Queensland, Australia
Place of Residence: Newport Beach, California, USA
Nationality: Australian
Height: 5ft 8in (1.73m)
Plays: Left-handed
Highest Ranking Reached: No. 3 (August 9, 1974)

Career Title Wins
Singles: 47
Doubles: 37

Grand Slam Highlights (only wins shown)
Singles
Australian—won 1960, 1962, 1969
French—won 1962, 1969
Wimbledon—won 1961, 1962, 1968, 1969
US—won 1962, 1969

Doubles
Australian—won (w/Mark) 1959, 1960, 1961, (w/Emerson) 1969
French—won (w/Emerson) 1961
Wimbledon—won (w/Emerson) 1971

Mixed Doubles
French—won (w/Hard) 1961
Wimbledon—won (w/Hard) 1959, 1960

Many consider Rod Laver to be the greatest tennis player of all time. In a career that spanned the amateur and professional eras, it did not matter whether he was playing as an amateur, contract professional or in the early days of the open era, he was dominant.

A sickly child born into the Australian bush, where his father farmed sheep, Laver learnt how to whip topspin ground strokes out on the family's antbed court. One day, his father decided to take him to one of the great Harry Hopman's clinics. Hopman took one look at the skinny little kid on the court and, rather sarcastically, said 'Okay, Rocket, let's see what you can do.' The name always stuck with him.

Hopman was impressed by what he saw. Although Laver, a slight, freckled red-head, looked ordinary off court, he became an intimidating presence on. He was strong, swinging hard and fast at every ball, and produced powerful shots on both flanks. He was also prepared to work hard in order to achieve results and, under the tutelage of Hopman, Laver's supreme craft was honed.

His first major triumph came in 1956, when he won the US Junior Championship at the age of 17. Three years later, he took his place among the world's best, winning the Australian Open singles and doubles titles, the first of the 20 major titles he was to win.

He also reached the 1958 Wimbledon final, the first of six in which he was to play. In all, he won four Wimbledon singles titles, in four straight entries into the competition. Having signed a professional contract in 1963, he was barred from the event for five years. If he had been eligible, that tally would surely have been higher.

Of course, Laver's unique claim to fame is that he won two Grand Slams, one as an amateur in 1962 and the other as a professional in 1969. Having kissed good-bye to his amateur status after the first, he became the undisputed king of the professional tour, but with the dawn of the open era in 1968, he was able to enter the majors again, allowing him to win his second.

The second was undoubtedly more satisfying because, unlike his 1962 Grand Slam, the events were open to all and the competition was much stronger. To top it all, during his 1969 Grand Slam, he created another piece of history by winning a total of 17 titles—an open era record that was only ever equalled by Guillermo Vilas in 1977.

Ivan Lendl

STATISTICS

Date of Birth: March 7, 1960
Place of Birth: Ostrava, Czechoslovakia
Place of Residence: Goshen, Connecticut, USA
Nationality: US
Height: 6ft 2in (1.88m)
Plays: Right-handed
Highest Ranking Reached: No. 1 (February 28, 1983)

Career Title Wins
Singles: 94
Doubles: 6

Grand Slam Highlights (wins only shown)
Singles
Australian—won 1989, 1990
French—won 1984, 1986, 1987
US—won 1985, 1986, 1987

Awards
ATP Tour Most Improved Player 1981
ATP Tour Player of the Year 1985, 1986, 1987

Ivan Lendl, like his compatriot Martina Navratilova, worked mechanically towards becoming the perfect tennis player and he came pretty close but, unfortunately, even the best laid plans can go awry. Despite 14 attempts, Lendl will always be remembered for his failure to win Wimbledon.

Lendl has excellent tennis pedigree. He was introduced to the game by his parents, Olga Lendlova, who was the driving force behind his early successes and had a national top three ranking, and his father Jiri, who reached No. 15 in the national rankings.

Lendl enjoyed a successful junior career, winning the boys' singles at Rome, Paris and Wimbledon in 1978, before turning professional. In two years, he had made his mark on the senior Tour, finishing in the top ten in 1980, having accrued a record 109 wins on the Tour and his first Tour title.

The following year, he reached his first Grand Slam final at the French Open, where he lost to Bjorn Borg in five sets. For a time, he appeared to be doomed to be a runner-up in Grand Slam events, as final finishes followed at the 1982 and 1983 US Open. That all changed in 1984, when he won the first of his Grand Slam titles at the French Open, having been two sets down to John McEnroe in the title match, and the following year, he won his first US Open title.

Four Grand Slam titles in 1986 and 1987 kept Lendl in the top spot which he had first captured in 1983, but his failure to win a major in 1988 resulted in him relinquishing his No. 1 ranking. In 1989, he won his first Tour title on grass, at Queen's, proving that he could triumph on all four surfaces—clay, carpet, grass and hard—but Wimbledon was the one major still to elude him.

In the very methodical manner in which he approached his tennis, Lendl decided to miss the French Open in 1990 to spend four weeks practising on grass for Wimbledon. Unfortunately, he still lost in the semi-finals. His baseline game, which relied on strength, topspin and determination, was not a pretty sight and was not suited to grass, but one could not help but admire Lendl for trying.

Back problems started to hamper his game in 1993, the first year in 13 that he did not finish in the top ten year end rankings. Matters did not improve in 1994, when he was forced to retire from four tournaments, and he finished outside the top 50 for the first time since 1978. At the beginning of 1995, Lendl retired, on doctor's orders.

Having settled in the United States (becoming an American citizen in 1992) he now lives in Connecticut, where—if his health allows—he will be found practising his golf swing.

Hana Mandlikova

STATISTICS

Date of Birth: February 19, 1962
Place of Birth: Prague, Czech Rep
Place of Residence: Prague, Czech Rep
Nationality: Australian
Height: 5ft 8in (1.73m)
Plays: Right-handed
Highest Ranking Reached: No. 3 (1984)

Career Title Wins
Singles: 27
Doubles: 6

Grand Slam Highlights
Singles
Australian—won 1980, 1987; SF 1985; QF 1979, 1981, 1988

French—won 1981; SF 1980, 1982, 1984, 1986; QF 1979, 1983, 1985
Wimbledon—runner-up 1981, 1986; SF 1984
US—won 1985; runner-up 1980, 1982; QF 1981, 1983, 1984

Doubles
French—runner-up (w/Kohde-Kilsch) 1984
Wimbledon—runner-up (w/Turnbull) 1986
US—won (w/Navratilova) 1989; runner-up (w/Turnbull) 1986

Awards
WTA Tour Most Improved Player Award 1980

Hana Mandlikova was a brilliant player who never fulfilled her potential. Sometimes, she played like a genius. At other times—when matches weren't going her way, when frustration set in, when she lost concentration—she played like a dog.

Mandlikova inherited her slender build from her father, Vilem Mandlik, 11-time national champion, who competed for Czechoslovakia in the 100m and 200m events in the 1956 and 1960 Olympics. A graceful athlete herself, she was quick around the court and, like her one-time compatriot Martina Navratilova, was keen to attack the net.

Mandlikova's talent was obvious at an early age. In 1978, a year in which she was runner-up to Tracy Austin in the Wimbledon girls' event, she was crowned ITF Junior World Champion. The following year, her first on the senior Tour, she won five events and broke into the top twenty.

She first peaked in late 1980/early 1981, when she reached the semi-finals of the US Open (losing in three sets to Chris Evert), and won both the Australian and French Opens. Inexplicably, she was not to win another major until 1985, making early round exits in most of the majors in between. At least

Mandlikova was consistent on one front. With Navratilova having defected to the United States, she led Czechoslovakia to three consecutive Federation Cup wins, in 1983-85.

Playing possibly the best tennis of her career, Mandlikova won the US Open in 1985, scoring a rare feat, back-to-back wins over Navratilova and Evert, en route to the title. In 1986, she also posted strong finishes at the French Open, reaching the semi-finals, and Wimbledon, where she lost in the final.

In 1986, she announced her marriage to a Czech-born Australian, Jan Sedlak, and became an Australian citizen in 1988. As if to prove her allegiance, she won the 1987 Australian Open, bringing Navratilova's 56 match-winning streak to an end. It was to be her last Grand Slam singles title, although she teamed up with Navratilova to win the US Open doubles in 1989.

A hamstring injury in 1988 meant that Mandlikova spent six months away from the Tour. In her second match back, she proved that she was still capable of great play by beating Evert. She retired in 1990. She now divides her time between coaching the Czech Jana Novotna and playing on the Virginia Slims Legends Tour.

John McEnroe

STATISTICS

Date of Birth: February 16, 1959
Place of Birth: Wiesbaden, Germany
Place of Residence: New York, New York and Malibu, California, USA
Nationality: US
Height: 5ft 11in (1.80m)
Plays: Left-handed
Highest Ranking Reached: No. 1 (March 3, 1980)

Career Title Wins
Singles: 77
Doubles: 77

Grand Slam Highlights wins only shown
Singles
Wimbledon—won 1981, 1983, 1984

US—won 1979-81, 1984

Doubles
Wimbledon—won (w/Fleming) 1979, 1981, 1983, 1984, (w/Stich) 1992
US—won (w/Fleming) 1979, 1981, 1983, (w/Woodforde) 1989

Mixed Doubles
French—won (w/Carillo) 1977

Awards
ATP Tour Player to Watch 1978
ATP Tour Player of the Year 1981, 1983, 1984
ATP Tour Doubles Team of the Year 1979, 1981, 1983, 1984

John McEnroe is one of the greatest players of the modern era. Unfortunately, he is also one of the most controversial, more likely to be remembered for his tantrums than his tennis.

Although scrawny, the left-handed McEnroe was a genius with a brilliant touch that enabled him to slice the ball right out of court on his service, and then to play a full range of shots, from whipped cross-courts to delicate drop shots. The histrionics he was to blame on a variety of problems, particularly the ineptitude of officials—"You cannot be serious" became a personal mantra.

McEnroe burst onto the tennis scene in 1977, winning both the junior boys' singles and the main Mixed Doubles title at the French Open. A few weeks later, he went on to became the first qualifier to reach the semifinals of Wimbledon, where he lost to Jimmy Connors. It was a record for an amateur in the open era. McEnroe then returned to Stanford, where he won the national student singles title in 1978. Later that year, he turned professional and joined the Tour. Within three years, he was No. 1, a ranking that he was to retain for a total of 170 weeks.

In 1979, he set an open era record with 27 overall tournament victories, winning a record total of 177 matches. One of the 10 singles titles he won was his first major singles title, the 1979 US Open, which he was to win three years running.

A match for which McEnroe is best remembered is one he lost: the epic 1980 Wimbledon final, in which he was beaten in five sets by Bjorn Borg. In a rematch the following year, the American gained his revenge, winning the first of three Wimbledon titles—the other two would come in 1983 and 1984.

In fact, McEnroe was almost unbeatable in 1984, winning 13 of the 15 tournaments he entered. One of the two matches he lost that year was the final of the French Open, when, two sets up against Ivan Lendl, his temper got the better of him. It was proof, however, that although he had his greatest successes on fast courts, he had the tenacity to do well on clay.

Of course McEnroe is also recognised as the best doubles player of all time, having been ranked No. 1 for a record 257 weeks. His peers used to say that it did not matter with whom McEnroe played, because he could have carried his side to victory on his own.

1985 was not a good year, as he lost his No. 1 ranking, and the following year he took an eight month break from the Tour. His comeback was not a great success, but he continued to play until 1992.

Thomas Muster

STATISTICS

Date of Birth: October 2, 1967
Place of Birth: Leibnitz, Austria
Place of Residence: Monte Carlo, Monaco
and Noosa Heads, Australia
Nationality: Austrian
Height: 5ft 11in (1.80m)
Plays: Left-handed
Highest Ranking Reached: No. 1
(February 12, 1996)

Career Title Wins
Singles: 42
Doubles: 1

Grand Slam Highlights
Australian—SF 1989, 1997; QF 1994
French—won 1995; SF 1990
US—QF 1993, 1994, 1996

Awards
ATP Tour Comeback Player of the Year
1990
ATP Tour Ironman Award 1995

The most impressive fact about Thomas Muster is not that he won the French Open in 1995, but that he is still playing tennis at all.

In March 1989, while in Miami, Muster was getting a sandwich out of the boot of his car, when he was hit by a drunk driver and the ligaments in his left knee were severed. On returning to Vienna to undergo surgery, he was informed that he would never play tennis again.

Muster, who has been quoted as saying he 'lives for tennis', decided otherwise. With the help of his coach, Ronnie Leitgeb, he went into rehabilitation almost immediately, going so far as to have a special chair built so that he could sit on the court with his left leg outstretched, while hitting practice balls. Within six months, Muster was back on the Tour.

As a junior, in 1985 Muster reached the finals of the French Open and the Orange Bowl. A year later, in his first season on the Tour, he won his first title. Solid results followed in 1987 and 1988, and the Austrian broke into the top twenty. In 1989, he became the first Austrian to reach the semi-finals of the Australian Open and to be ranked inside the top ten. Then, of course, came the fateful incident in Florida.

Amazingly, despite being away from the Tour, he finished 1990 ranked in the top ten. Title wins in Adelaide, Casablanca and Rome, plus final finishes in Monte Carlo and Munich, helped his cause.

The argument that many have levelled at Muster is that he can only play on one surface—clay—and that is certainly where he has achieved the vast majority of his tournament wins. In 1991, he captured two clay court titles; in 1992, he won three clay titles; in 1993, he led the Tour with 55 clay court wins; and in 1994, he won another three titles, all on clay.

Muster peaked in 1995, winning 12 titles, one of which was his first Grand Slam title, the French Open. Muster's marathon clay win started in Mexico City in February and lasted for 40 consecutive clay court matches, ending in July, when he lost in the first round at Gstaad.

The highlight of 1996 for Muster, other than another handful of clay court victories, was his elevation to the No. 1 ranking in February, making him (at 28 years 4 months) the second-oldest player ever to capture the top spot for the first time.

Following Muster's astounding results in 1995 and 1996, it was a different story in 1997, when he won two titles—on hard court—but struggled on clay, only achieving a mediocre 7-7 win-loss record for the year. Perhaps he was trying to combat the criticism and prove that he can win on all surfaces.

Ilie Nastase

STATISTICS

Date of Birth: July 19, 1946
Place of Birth: Bucharest, Romania
Place of Residence: New York, New York, USA
Nationality: Romanian
Height: 6ft 0in (1.83m)
Plays: Right-handed
Highest Ranking Reached: No. 1 (August 23, 1973)

Career Title Wins
Singles: 57
Doubles: 51

Grand Slam Highlights
Singles
French—won 1973; runner-up 1971; QF 1970, 1974, 1977
Wimbledon—runner-up 1972, 1976; QF 1977, 1978
US—won 1972; SF 1976; QF 1975

Doubles
French—won (w/Tiriac) 1970; runner-up (w/Connors) 1973
Wimbledon—won (w/Connors) 1973
US—won (w/Connors) 1975

Ilie the 'Bucharest Buffoon' Nastase was always a great entertainer—if he wasn't telling the Wimbledon crowd a joke, he was playing with an umbrella in his spare hand or a long blonde wig on his head. He was also, although the antics often overshadowed this fact, a great tennis player.

Nastase was the first Romanian of note to emerge on the international tennis scene. He first made headlines when he and compatriot Ion Tiriac reached the finals of the French Open doubles in 1966.

He then impressed on the Davis Cup competition, virtually carrying Romania to the final on three occasions, the first in 1969, followed by 1971 and 1972. Each time they lost to the United States.

In 1970, Nastase started to make advances on the Tour, winning the Italian Open and the US Indoor. His finest season, however, was in 1973, when he won the Italian and French Opens, plus another 13 tournaments, resulting in his No. 1 ranking in August.

His results in subsequent years were patchy. Nastase's weakness was that he allowed his temperament to get in the way of his playing. When he concentrated, he played like a gifted angel; when he allowed his mind to wander, he started to behave like a naughty schoolboy. His time on the Tour was, therefore, marred by a series of fines, disqualifications and suspensions.

At his best, Nastase introduced a touch of originality to the game and placed balls beautifully just beyond his opponent's reach. In defence, he could lob and retrieve brilliantly, being one of the fastest players among his peers. He was also capable of performing well on all surfaces although he achieved the majority of his tournament wins on clay: he won the US Open in 1972 and he reached two Wimbledon finals, in 1972 when he lost a splendid fluctuating five-set thriller against American Stan Smith and in 1976 when he lost disappointingly to the young Bjorn Borg, just starting his amazing Wimbledon winning run, in straight sets.

His brilliance inspired—perhaps not surprisingly given the brooding good looks of his youth—a generation of young Romanian players, all of whom were women: Virginia Ruzici, Florenza Mihai and Mariana Simionescu all reached the upper echelons of women's tennis in the 1970s.

These days, having failed to become Mayor of Bucharest in 1996, Nastase still competes on the men's Senior Tour, or should that read 'does his stand-up comic routine, interrupted by a little tennis?'

Martina Navratilova

STATISTICS

Date of Birth: October 18, 1956
Place of Birth: Prague, Czech Republic
Place of Residence: Aspen, Colorado, USA
Nationality: US
Height: 5ft 8in (1.73m)
Plays: Left-handed
Highest Ranking Reached: No. 1 (July 10, 1978)

Career Title Wins
Singles: 167
Doubles: 165

Grand Slam Highlights wins only shown
Singles
Australian—won 1981, 1983, 1985
French—won 1982, 1984
Wimbledon—won 1978-79, 1982-87, 1990
US—won 1983, 1984, 1986, 1987
Doubles
Australian—won (w/Nagelsen) 1980,
(w/Shriver) 1982, 1984, 1985, 1987-89
French—won (w/Evert) 1975, (w/A Smith)
1982, (w/Shriver) 1984-85, 1987-88,
(w/Temesvari) 1986
Wimbledon—won (w/Evert) 1976, (w/King)
1979, (w/Shriver) 1981-84, 1986
US—won (w/Stove) 1977, (w/King) 1978,
1980, (w/Shriver) 1983-84, 1986-87,
(w/Mandlikova) 1989, (w/G Fernandez) 1990
Mixed Doubles
French—won (w/Molina) 1974,
(w/Gunthardt) 1985
Wimbledon—won (w/McNamee) 1985,
(w/Woodforde) 1993, (w/Stark) 1995
US—won (w/Gunthardt) 1985,
(w/E Sanchez) 1987

Awards
WTA Tour Player of the Year 1978-79, 1982-86
WTA Tour Doubles Team of the Year
(w/Betty Stove) 1977, (w/Billie Jean Moffitt)
1978, 1979, (w/Pam Shriver) 1981-88

Many consider Martina Navratilova to be the best women's player of all time, because she was so prolific a winner for so long in an era in which standards were increasingly high.

It was Navratilova herself who helped improve those levels of play. With the aid of computer programming, she set about perfecting her work outs, practice sessions and diet—and thus forced other players to do the same if they were to have any hope of beating her.

Navratilova sprung to prominence at the age of 16, when, unseeded, she reached the quarter-finals of the 1973 French. Brought up on clay, she preferred to rush the net and, within two years, was ranked No. 2.

Her life changed dramatically when she defected at the US Open in 1975, becoming an American citizen in 1981. It was then that she adopted a more serious approach to her tennis. The hard work paid off when she won Wimbledon in 1978 and 1979, and finally overtook Evert as world No.1.

In 1980 and 1981, her dominance was challenged by Austin and Mandlikova, but in 1982, Navratilova returned to peak form. She won every major between Wimbledon 1983 and the Australian in 1985, except the 1984 Australian, thus securing a non-calendar Grand Slam.

1987 marked the arrival of Steffi Graf who would displace Navratilova as No. 1. In 1988 and 1989, the German picked up all the majors bar the 1989 French, but in 1990, was defeated by the American Zina Garrison in the semi-finals of Wimbledon, leaving the way clear for Navratilova to win a record-breaking ninth singles title.

Navratilova was never to win another singles major, although she did make the finals of the 1991 US and Wimbledon in 1994. She returned to her beloved Wimbledon in 1995, playing for fun in the mixed doubles with Jonathan Stark: they won the title!

Navratilova will also be remembered for her remarkable doubles partnership with Pam Shriver—they did not lose a match between April 1983 and July 1985, giving them a 109-match winning streak and a 1984 Grand Slam.

—John Newcombe

STATISTICS

Date of Birth: May 23, 1944
Place of Birth: Sydney, NSW, Australia
Place of Residence: Pymble, NSW, Australia
Nationality: Australian
Height: 6ft 1in (1.85m)
Plays: Right-handed
Highest Ranking Reached: No. 1 (June 3, 1974)

Career Title Wins
Singles: 32
Doubles: 41

Grand Slam Highlights wins only shown
Singles
Australian—won 1973, 1975

Wimbledon—won 1967, 1970, 1971
US—won 1967, 1973
Doubles
Australian—won (w/Roche) 1965, 1967, 1971, (w/Anderson) 1973, (w/Roche) 1976
French—won (w/Roche) 1967, 1969, (w/Okker) 1973
Wimbledon—won (w/Roche) 1965, (w/Fletcher) 1966, (w/Roche) 1968-70, 1974
US—won (w/Roche) 1967, (w/Taylor) 1971, (w/Davidson) 1973

Mixed Doubles
Australian—won (w/Smith) 1965
US—won (w/Smith) 1964

John Newcombe was not only a superb singles player, he also formed a formidable doubles partnership with his Australian compatriot, Tony Roche.

As a youngster, Newcombe was an all-round sportsman and it was not until the relatively late age of 17 that he decided to focus his energies on tennis. Coached by Harry Hopman, a major force in the game during the 1950s and 1960s, Newcombe served notice of his potential when, at 19, he was one of the youngest Australians ever to compete in the Davis Cup. Although beaten by the US that year, Newcombe became a Cup stalwart and helped Australia win the Cup from 1964 to 1967.

Like Laver, Newcombe's career spanned the transition from amateurism to professionalism and, as a result, they are the only two players to have won both Wimbledon and the US Open as amateurs and professionals.

Newcombe's first major victory was the 1965 Australian Open doubles, which he won with Roche. Predictably, his first Grand Slam singles title came at Wimbledon in 1967. His game was based on a very strong serve (probably the most powerful of the time) and accurate volleys, so it was perfectly suited to grass. In total, he would win the Wimbledon singles crown three times and could possibly have added another couple if the two bodies

with which he was associated, World Championship Tennis and the Association of Tennis Professionals, had not been in dispute with the International Tennis Federation (in 1972 and 1973 respectively), thus banning him from competition.

Newcombe added grass wins at the US and Australian Opens to his collection, but proved that he could also win on clay by taking the German Open in 1968 and the Italian Open in 1969.

As a doubles team, Newcombe and Roche were one of the greatest in the history of the game. They won Wimbledon five times together, a record in the 20th century until the Woodies won their fifth consecutive title in 1997; and with wins at the US, French and Australian Opens, they are one of just four teams to have captured every major doubles title. In addition, Newcombe captured another five Grand Slam titles with other partners, plus two mixed doubles titles with the great Margaret Smith.

Newcombe continued to play doubles at the Grand Slams for some time after he retired from singles. One of his last performances was at Wimbledon 1985, when he and American Andrea Leand had match points against the holders, Britain's John Lloyd and Wendy Turnbull of Australia.

Yannick Noah

STATISTICS

Date of Birth: May 18, 1960
Place of Birth: Sedan, France
Place of Residence: Paris, France
Nationality: French
Height: 6ft 4in (1.93m)
Plays: Right-handed
Highest Ranking Reached: No. 3 (July 7, 1986)

Career Title Wins
Singles: 23
Doubles: 16

Grand Slam Highlights
Singles
Australian—SF 1990; QF 1987
French—won 1983; QF 1981, 1982, 1984, 1987
US—QF 1982, 1984, 1989

Doubles
French—won (w/Leconte) 1984, (w/Forget) 1987
US—runner-up (w/Leconte) 1985

Awards
ATP Tour Sportsmanship Award 1986

The striking, dreadlocked Yannick Noah became the most famous tennis player in France since the demise of the 'Four Musketeers' when he won the 1983 French Open. Overnight, the French public took him to their hearts and elevated him to the status of superstar.

Born in Sedan, in eastern France, Noah spent his childhood in Cameroon, where he was 'discovered' by Arthur Ashe, who recommended him to the French tennis federation as a youngster worth developing.

The French Open junior champion in 1977, Noah quickly made his way through the senior rankings when he turned professional. With a stylish game that included powerful ground strokes and a gambling instinct to rush the net, where he combined a delicate touch and athletic, acrobatic volleying, a great future was predicted for young Yannick.

In the early years, he fulfilled that promise, winning three Tour events in 1979, reaching the final of the 1980 Italian Open, breaking into the top ten in 1982 (where he would remain for six years) and taking the title at the 1983 French Open, becoming the first Frenchman to win since Marcel Bernard in 1946.

Unfortunately, the adulation of his countrymen and the burden of expectation affected Noah badly. In 1984, he suffered from depression and his Tour results were disappointing. Marriage towards the end of the year, and the birth of a son, lifted his spirits and he fared better in 1985, winning the Italian Open, but he was then struck by injury problems.

Noah also enjoyed success as a doubles player, teaming with his fascinating but frustrating compatriot Henri Leconte to win the French Open in 1984 and to reach the finals of the 1985 US Open. In 1986, he was ranked No. 1 in doubles and the following year, he and Guy Forget were runners-up at the French Open.

Having finally stopped playing on the Tour, Noah was named the captain of the French Davis Cup team in 1991 and subsequently led them to their first title since 1932. He has also become something of a European pop star, having released several record albums and toured around the Continent.

Adriano Panatta

STATISTICS

Date of Birth: July 9, 1950
Place of Birth: Rome, Italy
Place of Residence: Florence, Italy
Nationality: Italian
Height: 6ft 0in (1.83m)
Plays: Right-handed
Highest Ranking Reached: No. 4 (August 24, 1976)

Career Title Wins
Singles: 10
Doubles: 18

Grand Slam Highlights
Singles
French—won 1976; SF 1973; QF 1972, 1977
Wimbledon—QF 1979

Adriano Panatta is probably remembered more for his good looks than for his tennis, but he was the best Italian player since Nicola Pietrangeli, who reached his peak in the late 1950s and early 1960s, winning the French Open in 1959 and 1960.

Panatta came from a family of tennis players and his younger brother, Claudio, played on the Tour from 1981 to 1989. They both reached the top ten—the only Italians to do so, but Adriano attained the higher ranking of No. 4 in 1976.

As with so many Italians, Panatta achieved his best results on clay. He was the only player ever to beat Bjorn Borg at the French Open, where the Swede had a 49-2 win-loss record, Panatta's two victories being recorded in 1973 and 1976.

Panatta reached his peak in 1976, when he won the Italian Open (having miraculously survived 11 match points against him when he played the Czech Pavel Hutka in the first round), followed by the French Open, compiling a 45-15 match record that year.

Handsome and charismatic, the six foot Adonis was adored by the Italian public. Every year at the Italian Open's Il Foro Italico they would inspire him with their feverish chanting of 'AD-REE-ANNO!' They carried him to the final of the Italian Open again in 1978, but Borg finally gained his revenge, winning a classic five set final.

It is a pity the Foro Italico crowds did not follow Panatta around the world, because he was prone to laziness and could have achieved so much more if he had only put a little more time and effort into his practice and play. With his powerful serve, whipped forehand and brilliant diving saves at the net, for which he was nicknamed 'The Goalkeeper', Panatta had all the requirements to do well.

He could even, when he put his mind to it, play on surfaces other than clay, reaching the quarter-finals at Wimbledon in 1979 and winning the British Hard Court title in 1973.

In the Davis Cup, Panatta led Italy to their one and only title win when he was in form in 1976, and also helped the Italian team reach the final on three other occasions (1977, 1979 and 1980). In the modern era, he is one of the few players to have played 100 Davis Cup rubbers (63 singles, 37 doubles), spanning from 1970 to 1982.

Mary Pierce

STATISTICS

Date of Birth: January 15, 1975
Place of Birth: Montreal, Canada
Place of Residence: Paris, France and Bradenton, Florida, USA
Nationality: French
Height: 5ft 10.5in (1.80m)
Plays: Right-handed
Highest Ranking Reached: No. 3 (January 30, 1995)

Career Title Wins
Singles: 8
Doubles: 3

Grand Slam Highlights
Singles
Australian—won 1995; runner-up 1997; QF 1993
French—runner-up 1994
Wimbledon—QF 1996
US—QF 1994

Awards
WTA Tour Most Improved Player 1994
WTA Tour Comeback Player of the Year 1997

Mary Pierce is famous for three things: her looks, her schizophrenic father and her tennis. Unfortunately, although she has had her moments on court, she has failed to fulfil her real potential to date, so will probably be remembered in the future for her looks and her father.

Slim, tall, with long blonde hair, Pierce would be a tennis photographer's dream with her natural looks alone, but when she teams these with figure-hugging, skimpy halter-neck dresses from her sponsor, Nike, the media corps talks of little else.

Pierce was introduced to tennis at the age of ten by her father Jim. Just four years later, as an American, she made her professional debut aged 14 years 2 months. In March 1990, Pierce claimed the French nationality of her mother in order to qualify for national training assistance, something that her father (who was then her coach) claimed she had been denied in the United States.

In 1991, an unseeded Pierce won her first major title and started a steady climb up through the women's rankings. En route, she had a restraining order placed on her father, whom she claimed had hit her.

She found a new coach in Nick Bollettieri and reached her first Grand Slam final at the 1994 French Open. During the event, Pierce made history by becoming the first player to lose only 10 games (four won by Steffi Graf in the semi-finals) in six rounds. At the last hurdle, she lost the title to Spaniard Arantxa Sanchez Vicario 6-4, 6-4. Nonetheless, she made her first top ten appearance with her ranking jumping to the heights of No. 7.

In 1995, Pierce finally won her first Grand Slam title, capturing the Australian Open and her ranking climbed to a career-high No. 3. Since then, she has split with Bollettieri and her results have been patchy, flashes of brilliance contrasting with poor performances.

The highlights have included Pierce's unseeded appearance in the final of the 1997 Australian Open, having beaten four seeded players in early rounds; final finishes in 1997 in Amelia Island and Berlin following wins over three players ranked in the top ten in both events; and a win at the 1997 Italian Open. The final finish in Berlin saw Pierce return to the top ten.

Patrick Rafter

STATISTICS

Date of Birth: December 28, 1972
Place of Birth: Mount Isa, Queensland, Australia
Place of Residence: Pembroke, Bermuda
Nationality: Australian
Height: 6ft 1in (1.85m)
Plays: Right-handed
Highest Ranking Reached: No. 2 (November 17, 1997)

Career Title Wins
Singles: 2
Doubles: 5

Grand Slam Highlights
Singles
French—SF 1997
US—won 1997

Doubles
Wimbledon—SF (w/Philippoussis) 1996
US—SF (w/Philippoussis) 1996

Awards
ATP Tour Player to Watch 1993

Having been touted as a great prospect for many years, Patrick Rafter finally proved his mettle by winning the 1997 US Open.

Rafter started playing tennis with his father and brothers at the age of five. As the third youngest of nine children, he was never short of someone to play with or coach him, as his elder brother Geoff, along with Tony Roche, does now.

Since turning professional, he has risen steadily through the ranks. In 1991, his first year on the Tour, he was a Challenger finalist and in 1993 made his first Tour semi-final, defeating world No. 1 Pete Sampras to claim his first win over a top ten player. The following year, Rafter won his first career singles title and posted semi-final or better results in four other events.

In 1995, he broke into the top twenty for the first time in both singles and doubles. Most of his impressive doubles results were racked up with Mark Philippoussis, another highly rated Australian player.

Unfortunately, towards the end of the year, Rafter's progress was hampered by surgery to repair torn cartilage in his right wrist.

Rafter continued to battle injury throughout early 1996, but in April returned to the Tour, reaching the quarter-finals of tournaments played on three different surfaces—clay, grass and carpet. He and Philippoussis also reached the semi-finals of Wimbledon and the US Open.

1997 was Rafter's best year yet. He played well on all surfaces, reaching six Tour finals. He also won his first Grand Slam, the US Open, becoming the first Australian since John Newcombe in 1973 to win the title. Following his victory, his ranking jumped from No. 14 to No. 3 and he ended the year one place higher at No. 2.

Another good season with Philippoussis in doubles meant that he was ranked No. 12 in doubles at the year end.

The year was not, however, without its mishaps. Early in the year, he admitted walking on to court to play a Davis Cup doubles tie while still drunk from the previous night's partying. Perhaps that is part of the reason why Rafter has not been more consistently successful, but also part of the reason why he is universally popular.

People can associate with him because he enjoys nothing better than a night out having a good time, he is certainly not just another tennis machine. Of course, his good looks also attract legions of adoring female fans.

Marcelo Rios

STATISTICS

Date of Birth: December 26, 1975
Place of Birth: Santiago, Chile
Place of Residence: Santiago, Chile
Nationality: Chilean
Height: 5ft 8in (1.73m)
Plays: Left-handed
Highest Ranking Reached: No. 1 (End of March, 1998)

Career Title Wins
Singles: 5
Doubles: 1

Grand Slam Highlights
Singles
Australian—QF 1997
US—QF 1997

When Marcelo Rios first appeared on the tennis scene, he was compared with Andre Agassi because of his long flowing locks. A few years later, a comparison with John McEnroe seems more appropriate, given both players' ability to court controversy. Whether he is ever going to be a great tennis player seems almost irrelevant.

Rios had a very successful junior career, capturing the US Open junior title and finishing 1993 as the No. 1 ranked player in the world. In 1994, his first year on the Tour, he won his first Challenger title and rose more than 400 places in the rankings. The following year, he captured three Tour titles. At one, in Amsterdam, he had to qualify because his ranking was still too low and then dropped only one set en route to the title.

By spring 1996, Rios had become the first Chilean to make it into the top ten—a feat which he achieved faster than either Andre Agassi or Pete Sampras. His meteoric rise was attributed to his supreme talent, but it left the critics wondering whether his 'bad' attitude would allow him to stay there.

On Tour, Rios—known as 'El Chino' (The Chinaman) in Chile because of his slightly Oriental looks—has a reputation for being a difficult character; he is aloof with other players in the locker room; refuses all requests from the press to be interviewed; and has been through coaches at the rate of knots. His favourite saying is 'I don't care'.

His critics argued that he needed to tighten his concentration and determination if he was to succeed. This Rios appears to have done. In 1997, he remained in the top ten all but six weeks, winning the Monte Carlo title and reaching four other finals. He was also the only player to reach the fourth round or better of all the four Grand Slam tournaments.

At the beginning of 1998, he went one stage better, reaching the final of the Australian Open where he lost in straight sets to the Czech Petr Korda. At the end of March, at the Lipton Championships in Florida's Key Biscayne, Rios achieved the ultimate tennis player's dream, when he was crowned No.1 in the world, thus ending Sampras's 102-week reign at the top of the rankings. Ironically, Rios reached the top by beating Agassi, with whom he has so often been compared, in straight sets (7-5, 6-3, 6-4) in the final.

Almost inevitably, Rios's achievement was shrouded in controversy. Many believe he has no claim to the No.1 crown because he has yet to win a Grand Slam title—in contrast, Sampras has won ten majors.

Ken Rosewall

STATISTICS

Date of Birth: November 2, 1934
Place of Birth: Sydney, New South Wales, Australia
Place of Residence: Turramurra, New South Wales, Australia
Nationality: Australian
Height: 5ft 7in (1.70m)
Plays: Right-handed
Highest Ranking Reached: No. 2 (April 30, 1975)

Career Title Wins
Singles: 32
Doubles: 18

Grand Slam Highlights
Singles
Australian—won 1953, 1955, 1971, 1972; runner-up 1956; SF 1976, 1977; QF 1977
French—won 1953, 1968; runner-up 1969

Wimbledon—runner-up 1954, 1956, 1970, 1974; SF 1971
US—won 1956, 1970; runner-up 1955, 1974; SF 1968, 1973

Doubles
Australia—won (w/Hoad) 1953, 1956, (w/Davidson) 1972; runner-up (w/Hoad) 1955, (w/Stolle) 1969
French—won (w/Hoad) 1953, (w/Stolle) 1968; runner-up (w/Hoad) 1954
Wimbledon—won (w/Hoad) 1953, 1956; runner-up (w/Fraser) 1955, (w/Stolle) 1968, 1970
US—won (w/Hoad) 1956, (w/Stolle) 1969; runner-up (w/Laver) 1973

Mixed
Wimbledon—runner-up (w/Osborne) 1954
US—won (w/Osborne) 1956; runner-up (w/Osborne) 1954

Nicknamed 'Muscles', because of his compact muscular frame, Ken Rosewall is one of the greatest little men ever to play the game. He achieved amazing results spanning three decades and three eras: amateur, contract professional and open.

He grew up in Sydney, the son of a grocer. As a youngster he was a left-hander, but his father taught him to play right-handed and he developed one of the strongest backhands of the era.

Rosewall burst on to the tennis scene in 1952 and a year later captured his first two Grand Slam titles, the Australian and French Opens. Having won the 1956 US Open, he turned professional and continued on his winning ways, picking up the London Professional title in 1957, 1960, 1961, 1962 and 1963. He also won the US Professional title in 1963 and 1965.

In April 1968, he won the British Hard Courts, the world's first open event, which was played in Bournemouth and, later that year, won the French Open, which he had last won 15 years earlier.

In ensuing years, he won all the Grand Slam titles (in singles and doubles) except at Wimbledon. In the process, he set some impressive records with regard to significant victories over a long span of time: he won the US Open 14 years after he had first taken the title; 19 years after winning the Australian Open, he did it again; and 20 years after appearing in a Wimbledon final, he found himself in the same position again.

At the end of 1977, he was still ranked in the top 15, having won two tournaments that year. His last victory was in Hong Kong, two weeks after his 43rd birthday.

Rosewall proved that it wasn't necessary to be tall or to have a great service to succeed. Magnificent anticipation, perfect balance, speed around the court and excellent volleys were his winning tools.

Greg Rusedski

STATISTICS

Date of Birth: September 6, 1973
Place of Birth: Montreal, Quebec, Canada
Place of Residence: London, England
Nationality: British
Height: 6ft 4in (1.90m)
Plays: Left-handed
Highest Ranking Reached: No. 4 (October 6, 1997)

Career Title Wins
Singles: 5
Doubles: 2

Grand Slam Highlights
Singles
Wimbledon—QF 1997
US—runner-up 1997

Greg Rusedski, the former Canadian, inveigled his way into the British public's hearts by surviving to the fourth round of Wimbledon in 1995, the same year that he became a British citizen.

Since turning professional in 1990, Rusedski has made steady progress through the rankings. In 1992, he won his first Challenger title in Newcastle, followed in 1993 by his first Tour title in Newport and a final finish in Beijing (when he beat two top ten players, Dutchman Richard Krajicek and Michael Chang).

In 1994, Rusedski made the third round of the French Open, his best Grand Slam finish at the time, and won his first Tour doubles title in Newport.

1995 was a big year for Rusedski. In June, he gained British nationality on the strength of his mother having been born in Dewsbury, Yorkshire (his father is originally from Germany). A few weeks later he wowed the Wimbledon crowds by reaching the fourth round and sent them into a frenzy be unravelling his headband to reveal a Union Jack. It is not just the dramatics, however, that endear him to the public, it is also the ready smile on his lips, the willingness to talk to the media and the constant encouragement of junior players.

He was not so warmly welcomed by some of the other British tennis players, who feared for the loss of their Davis Cup squad places, but they had no right to complain.

Rusedski has had the right of dual Canadian/British nationality since birth and has lived in London since 1991, when he met his long term English girlfriend, Lucy Connors, while she was a ball girl at a match he was playing in Surrey's Thames Ditton.

After all the summer excitement, Rusedski moved on to play in Asia, where he took a Tour title in Seoul, and then to North America, where he made the final in Coral Springs. At the end of the year, he became the first British player since John Lloyd in 1985 to finish in the top 50.

The following year, Rusedski's success spurred other British players, particularly Tim Henman, on to greater things and for the first time since 1977, Britain had two players in the top 50.

Meanwhile, Rusedski continued to do well, winning the event in Beijing and reaching a handful of semi-finals in Tour competition. A major factor in his victories is his powerful serve—he currently holds the Tour record for the fastest serve hit, at 143mph.

In 1997, Rusedski—still only 24 years old—broke into the top ten despite missing two months early in the year because of an injured wrist.

He won two Tour titles in six finals, one of which was at the US Open, his first Grand Slam final, when he lost to Patrick Rafter in four sets while suffering from a heavy head cold. He was the first British player to reach the US final since Fred Perry in 1936.

Gabriela Sabatini

STATISTICS

Date of Birth: May 16, 1970
Place of Birth: Buenos Aires, Argentina
Place of Residence: Buenos Aires, Argentina
and Key Biscayne, Florida, USA
Nationality: Argentinean
Height: 5ft 9in (1.75m)
Plays: Right-handed
Highest Ranking Reached: No. 3 (Feb 1989)

Career Title Wins
Singles: 27
Doubles: 12

Grand Slam Highlights
Singles
Australian—SF 1989, 1992-94; QF 1991

French—SF 1985, 1987, 1988, 1991, 1992;
QF 1993, 1995
Wimbledon—runner-up 1991; SF 1986,
1990, 1992; QF 1987, 1993, 1995
US—won 1990; runner-up 1988; SF 1989,
1994, 1995; QF 1987, 1991, 1992, 1993

Doubles
French—runner-up (w/Graf) 1986, 1987,
1989
Wimbledon—won (w/Graf) 1988

Awards
WTA Tour Most Impressive Newcomer
Award 1985
WTA Most Improved Player Award 1991

Gabriela Sabatini, the leggy, dark-haired beauty from Argentina, was a sponsor's dream. She was also a very good tennis player, although some would argue that she failed to fulfil her potential.

Sabatini began playing tennis at the age of seven, inspired by the great Guillermo Vilas: she even went as far as to copy his backhand. At the age of 13 years 7 months 1week, she became the youngest player to win the Orange Bowl and in 1984 was the World Junior No. 1.

The same year, she made her first impact on the professional Tour at Hilton Head, where, due to rain, she had to play three matches in one day, beating American Pam Shriver in the quarter-finals and Manuela Maleeva of Switzerland in the semi-finals, before losing the final to Chris Evert. Her ranking jumped from No. 33 to No. 18.

In 1985, aged just 15, she reached the last four of the French Open, becoming the youngest player at the time to get to that stage. Once again, she lost to Evert.

Soon after, Steffi Graf rose to prominence on the Tour and it was expected that the two would enjoy a great rivalry, but it was not to be. Although Sabatini was ranked in the top ten from 1986 to 1992, peaking at No. 3 in 1989, she only captured one Grand Slam title, the US Open 1990. Coached by Brazilian Carlos Kirmayr, Sabatini attacked at every opportunity and beat Graf 6-2, 7-6 (7-4) to become the lowest seed (No. 5) for 22 years to win the title and the first female from Argentina to win a Grand Slam event.

It was a victory that the 'The Divine Argentine', as the press took to calling her, could not repeat. In the Wimbledon final of 1991, Sabatini — once again playing Graf— was up 6-5, 30-15 in the final set, when she lost her bottle and thus the title to the German.

In 1996, Sabatini spent three months away from the Tour with a pulled stomach muscle. Soon after her return, she announced her retirement and, on October 15, played her last match—a first round loss to a rejuvenated Jennifer Capriati.

Still only 26 years old, Sabatini could well afford to retire, having made nearly US$8 million in on-court earnings and many, many more millions in endorsements from, among others, Sergio Tacchini and RayBan. She now lives mostly in Florida, where she spent her formative years, but she does have a full working ranch in Argentina.

Pete Sampras

STATISTICS

Date of Birth: August 12, 1971
Place of Birth: Washington, DC, USA
Place of Residence: Tampa, Florida, USA
Nationality: US
Height: 6ft 1in (1.85m)
Plays: Right-handed
Highest Ranking Reached: 1 (April 12, 1993)

Career Title Wins
Singles: 52
Doubles: 2

Grand Slam Highlights
Australian—won 1994, 1997; runner-up 1995; SF 1993
French—SF 1996; QF 1992, 1993, 1994
Wimbledon—won 1993, 1994, 1995, 1997; SF 1992; QF 1996
US—won 1990, 1993, 1995, 1996; runner-up 1992; QF 1991

Awards
ATP Tour Most Improved Player 1990
ATP Tour Player of the Year 1993, 1994, 1995, 1996

Many consider Pete Sampras to be the best tennis player of all time—although he will have to play successfully for a few more years before that claim can be substantiated.

Sampras started playing tennis at the age of seven, inspired by the great Rod Laver (with whom he is often compared). His first success actually came in doubles, when he teamed with Jim Courier in 1989 to win the Italian Open.

1990 was a breakthough year for Sampras. He won his first Tour event and his first Grand Slam title, taking the US Open with wins over Ivan Lendl, John McEnroe and Andre Agassi to become the youngest men's champion at 19 years 28 days.

He was not to win another major until Wimbledon 1993, but since then Sampras has been close to invincible at all the Grand Slam events that are not played on clay: he has never won the French Open. That is not to say he cannot play on clay—he captured his first clay court event in 1992 and won the Italian Open in 1994—but his game is better suited to fast, particularly grass, surfaces.

In 1993, Sampras became the 11th player to be ranked No. 1 on the men's Tour and the following year he held the top spot for the entire calendar year (the first person to do so since Lendl in 1987) staying there for 82 weeks from September 1993 to April 1995. He has also finished in the top spot at the end of every year since 1993, only the second person (the other is Jimmy Connors) to achieve a five-year streak.

Remarkably, Sampras kept claiming victories throughout 1995, when his coach Tim Gullikson was severely ill with a brain tumour, and 1996, when Gullikson died in May. In 1995, he won Wimbledon (for the third year running) and the US Open for the third time. At the French Open 1996, three weeks after his coach died, Sampras had his best showing ever, reaching the semi-finals before losing to the eventual winner, Yevgeny Kafelnikov.

Although his 25-match winning streak at Wimbledon ended in the 1996 quarter-finals, where he was beaten by the eventual champion Richard Krajicek of the Netherlands, Sampras enjoyed a successful hard court season, winning his eighth Grand Slam title at the US Open.

At the end of 1997, having won eight titles including the Australian Open and Wimbledon during the year, Sampras had been ranked No. 1 for 91 weeks running. With 10 Grand Slam titles to his name, he is now within striking distance of Rod Laver's record 12 Grand Slam singles titles.

Arantxa Sanchez Vicario

STATISTICS

Date of Birth: December 18, 1971
Place of Birth: Barcelona, Spain
Place of Residence: Andorra
Nationality: Spanish
Height: 5ft 6.5in (1.69 m)
Plays: Right-handed
Highest Ranking Reached: No. 1
(February 6, 1995)

Career Title Wins
Singles: 24
Doubles: 55

Grand Slam Highlights
Singles
Australian—runner-up 1994, 1995; SF
1991, 1992, 1993; QF 1996

French—won 1989, 1994; runner-up
1991, 1995, 1996; SF 1992, 1993; QF
1987, 1988, 1997
Wimbledon—runner-up 1995, 1996;
SF 1997; QF 1989, 1991
US—won 1994; runner-up 1992; SF
1990, 1993; QF 1989, 1991, 1997

Awards
WTA Tour Most Impressive Newcomer
1987
WTA Tour Most Improved Player 1988,
1989
WTA Tour Diamond Aces 1995
WTA Tour Doubles Team of the Year
(w/Jana Novotna) 1996

Arantxa Sanchez-Vicario is the most successful of a successful family of tennis players: both her brothers, Emilio and Javier, have prospered on the men's Tour and her sister, Marisa, played collegiate tennis.

She started playing tennis aged four and, when just 16, won her first professional tournament, the 1988 Belgian Open. In the same year, she upset clay court specialist Chris Evert 6-1, 7-6 (7-4) in a tiebreak in the third round of the French Open.

Exactly a year later, she beat Steffi Graf in the final to become the first Spanish woman to win the French Open. At that time, she was the youngest ever French champion at 17 years 6 months, a record topped by Monica Seles in 1990, when she was only 16 years 6 months old.

A valiant fighter, Sanchez-Vicario always appears to have boundless energy. Not only does she scamper around the court, endlessly retrieving balls which seem lost causes, but she is also one of a handful of top players to have reached the top in both singles and doubles. As a result, she plays more matches than most. In 1994, for example, the Spaniard swept the singles and doubles titles at seven Tour events.

1994, in general, was a big year for Sanchez-Vicario. Along with Sergi Brugera, she completed the first Spanish Grand Slam singles titles sweep at the French Open and then became the first Spanish woman to win the US Open. At the latter, she won the singles and doubles titles too, the first person to achieve this feat since Martina Navratilova in 1987.

In February 1996, Sanchez-VIcario became the sixth female player since computer rankings began in 1975, to hold the No. 1 singles ranking and the first Spaniard—male or female—to reach the top spot. A week later, she became the first player simultaneously to hold No. 1 singles and doubles ranking since Navratilova in 1987.

Since that peak, Sanchez-Vicario's results have been disappointing, but she is still only aged 26 and she should have a few years left on the Tour to regain her enthusiasm and win more titles.

Monica Seles

STATISTICS

Date of Birth: December 2, 1973
Place of Birth: Novi Sad, Yugoslavia
Place of Residence: Sarasota, Florida, USA
Nationality: US
Height: 5ft 10.5in (1.79 m)
Plays: Left-handed
Highest Ranking Reached: No. 1 (March 11, 1991)

Career Title Wins
Singles: 41
Doubles: 4

Grand Slam Highlights
Singles
Australian—won 1991, 1992, 1993, 1996

French—won 1990, 1991, 1992; SF 1989, 1997; QF 1996
Wimbledon—runner-up 1992; QF 1990
US—winner 1991, 1992; runner-up 1995, 1996; QF 1997

Doubles
Australian—SF 1991 (w/A Smith)

Awards
WTA Tour Most Improved Player 1990
WTA Tour Player of the Year 1991, 1992
WTA Tour Comeback Player of the Year 1995
WTA Tour Most Exciting Player 1995, 1997

From the moment she joined the women's professional tennis tour, it was apparent that Monica Seles was no ordinary player. In 1989, in only her second tournament as a pro, she upset Chris Evert to win an event in Houston.

Mustering all her energies behind her double-fisted ground strokes, Seles would pounce on every ball, unleashing her trademark grunt and, more often than not, a pinpoint accurate winner from the baseline. In addition, her mental toughness was legendary.

Off court, Seles had the 'X' factor attributed to all stars. Gushing sentences delivered in her staccato voice and, inevitably, followed by high-pitched giggles, endeared her to all those who came into contact with her, but—at the same time—she maintained an air of mystique that made her both enigmatic and fascinating.

Seles managed to rack up a series of firsts, including youngest player to win a Grand Slam (1990 French) and, at 17 years 3 months 9 days the youngest No. 1-ranked player in tennis history, although both records have now been surpassed by Martina Hingis.

It is probably, however, for her rivalry with Steffi Graf that she will best be remembered. On March 11, 1991, just two years after turning pro, she ended Steffi Graf's record 186-week dominance in the No. 1 spot, marking the start of a fascinating battle between the two players. In 1991 and 1992, she reached all but one tournament final, and won all the majors in which she played except Wimbledon 1992, when Graf maintained her dominance on grass.

Unfortunately, Seles's career was cruelly brought to a halt while competing in Hamburg on April 30, 1993, when, during a changeover, she was stabbed in the back by Günter Parche, a crazy German fan of Graf's. While the physical wound was not that serious, the psychological damage inflicted was severe.

It was not until the 1995 Canadian Open, 28 months later, that Seles returned to the tour. Remarkably, she won the event, beating Amanda Coetzer 6-0, 6-1 in the final. In her second tournament back, the US Open, she reached the final again, but this time she lost a thrilling match to her old adversary Graf.

Although Seles returned to the tour with enthusiasm and infectious giggle intact, as well as a stronger serve, nagging injuries and her father's battle against cancer have meant that her appearances have been few and far between.

—Stan Smith

STATISTICS

Date of Birth: December 4, 1946
Place of Birth: Pasadena, California, USA
Place of Residence: Hilton Head, South Carolina, USA
Nationality: US
Height: 6ft 3in (1.90m)
Plays: Right-handed
Highest Ranking Reached: No. 3 (August 23, 1973)

Career Title Wins
Singles: 39
Doubles: 61

Grand Slam Highlights
Singles
French—QF 1970, 1971
Wimbledon—won 1972; runner-up 1971; SF 1974

US—won 1971; SF 1973; QF 1970, 1972, 1974

Doubles
Australian—won (w/Lutz) 1970
French—runner-up (w/Gorman) 1971, (w/Lutz) 1971
Wimbledon—runner-up (w/Van Dillen) 1972, (w/Lutz) 1974, 1980, 1981
US—won (w/Lutz) 1968, 1974, 1978, 1980; runner-up (w/Van Dillen) 1971, (w/Lutz) 1979.

Awards
ATP Tour Doubles Team of the Year (w/Bob Lutz) 1980
ATP Tour Sportsmanship Award 1979
ATP Tour Humanitarian of the Year (w/Margie Smith) 1985

Stan Smith, while never one of the game's most exciting players, will always be remembered for his faultless sportsmanship, as well as his strong serve and volleying capabilities.

An All-American at the University of Southern California, Smith won the US Intercollegiate singles in 1968, as well as the doubles with his long-term doubles partner Bob Lutz in 1967 and 1968. In 1969, he also won the US National Championships.

1971 was a breakthrough year for Smith: he was the runner-up at Wimbledon and won the US Open, beating Czech Jan Kodes in the final, which had the distinction of being the first American major to end in a tiebreaker.

In 1972, Smith went one better at Wimbledon, beating Ilie Nastase in a classic five setter that ranks as one of the outstanding finals of the modern era and the first to be played on the second Sunday of the tournament. Without detracting from his win, because just beating the Romanian was quite an achievement, 1972 was the year that those

contracted to World Championship Tennis were not allowed to compete, so the field was weaker than it could have been.

Smith would win no more major singles titles, but with Lutz he formed one of the strongest doubles teams of the 1970s. Together they won five Grand Slam titles, four of which were at the US Open and the US National titles when it was played on four different surfaces—grass, clay, hard and carpet.

In all, Smith won 100 titles (39 singles and 61 doubles) making him one of the few players in the modern era to have scored a century.

One of the greatest matches Smith played was away from the Tour, while on Davis Cup duty. In front of a partisan crowd in Bucharest on clay, he managed to beat both Nastase (in straight sets) and Ion Tiriac (in a tense five sets) to help the Americans win the Cup for the fifth year running. Later, he would admit that in order to cut out all the distractions, he had had to 'concentrate so hard I got a headache'.

Guillermo Vilas

STATISTICS

Date of Birth: August 17, 1952
Place of Birth: Buenos Aires, Argentina
Place of Residence: Buenos Aires, Argentina
Nationality: Argentinean
Height: 5ft 11in (1.80m)
Plays: Left-handed
Highest Ranking Reached: No. 2 (April 30, 1975)

Career Title Wins
Singles: 62
Doubles: 14

Grand Slam Highlights
Singles
Australian—won 1978, 1979; runner-up 1977; SF 1980
French—won 1977; runner-up 1975, 1978, 1982; QF 1976, 1979, 1980, 1983, 1986
Wimbledon—QF 1975, 1976
US—won 1977; SF 1975, 1976, 1982

Awards
ATP Tour Most Improved Player 1974

Guillermo Vilas is the greatest player to have emerged from South America in the modern era, although Chile's Marcelo Rios has recently been pushing for that title.

Nicknamed the 'Young Bull of the Pampas', he first gained notice in 1973, when he beat the defending champion, Spain's Andres Gimeno, in the second round of the French Open.

By the end of 1974, he was ranked No. 4 and for the next decade, he would remain in the top ten.

With his ever present head band and flowing locks, he epitomised strength, fitness, endurance and patience (essential on his favoured clay courts), and it was to him that a whole generation of Latin American players—including the great Gabriela Sabatini—looked for inspiration.

Vilas peaked in 1977, winning 17 tournaments (including the French and US Open titles) and tying Rod Laver's record for most titles in 12 months. Up until the US Open, he was known for outlasting opponents with high-rolling topspin shots from the back of the court, but in the final (played on the grass of Forest Hills) he startled Jimmy Connors by changing tactics and attacking the net to ensure the title was his.

Although he was not a natural grass court player, more titles were to come his way. He won the Australian Open in 1978 and 1979, when it was still played at Kooyang on grass.

Towards the end of his prominence, Vilas almost won a second French Open in 1982, when he reached the final, but he was beaten by a young, unheralded kid from Sweden, Mats Wilander, who effectively beat him at his own baseline, clay court game.

Vilas's career slumped in 1983, when it was alleged that he had accepted an illegal guarantee to play in a tournament in Rotterdam, but he made something of a comeback in 1986, when he reached the quarterfinals of the French Open.

As recently as 1992, Vilas was still playing satellites (the lowest rung of the men's professional tennis circuit, below Challengers and Tour events), purely for the love of the game. Since 1993, he has become a mainstay of the Senior Tour, where he has renewed old rivalries with Jimmy Connors and Bjorn Borg, among others.

Virginia Wade

STATISTICS

Date of Birth: July 10, 1945
Place of Birth: Bournemouth, England
Place of Residence: New York, New York, USA
Nationality: British
Height: 5ft 8in (1.73m)
Plays: Right-handed
Highest Ranking Reached: No. 2 (November 1975)

Career Title Wins
Singles: 55
Doubles: 16

Grand Slam Highlights
Singles
Australian—won 1972; QF 1973
French—QF 1970, 1972
Wimbledon—won 1977; SF 1974, 1976, 1978; QF 1967, 1972, 1973, 1975, 1979, 1983
US—won 1968; SF 1969, 1970, 1975; QF 1966, 1972, 1973, 1977, 1979

Doubles
Australian—won 1973
French—won 1973; runner-up 1979
Wimbledon—runner-up 1970
US—won 1973, 1975; runner-up 1969, 1970, 1972, 1976

Awards
WTA Tour Player of the Year 1977

Virginia Wade is the most successful and best-known women's player to emerge from Britain in the modern era.

Born in England, Wade grew up and learnt to play tennis in South Africa, where her father was the Archdeacon of Durban. At the age of 15, she returned to England to study and would later combine university studies with competitive play, on occasion literally. During the 1966 Wightman Cup, Wade sat her finals in a special room set up at the All England Club.

The next year, Wade entered the top ten and would remain there for 13 straight years, peaking at No. 2 in 1968. Her career began just as the amateur era was drawing to a close and the open era was beginning, which enabled her to achieve two firsts. In 1968, as an amateur, she won the inaugural open event, the British Hard Court, at Bournemouth and had to turn down the first prize of £300; five months later, as a professional, she won the inaugural US Open (and US$6,000) by beating the favourite, Billie Jean Moffitt.

Wade stumbled through a few years before meeting with more success. At the Australian Open 1972, she beat Evonne Goolagong, using her usual arsenal of weapons: a sliced backhand approach shot and excellent volleys, both of which were well suited to the grass at Kooyang.

Although Wade could be erratic in her early days on the Tour, she matured into a solid match player after competing in the World Team Tennis league in the United States. In all, she won 55 titles, making her the most successful of all British women players. She also formed a good doubles partnership with Margaret Smith, and together they won the Australian, French and US Opens.

Her greatest moment came at Wimbledon in 1977, when 'Our Ginny' surprised her many fans by winning the ladies' singles title. Having beaten former champion Chris Evert in the semi-finals, she beat Betty Stove of the Netherlands in a tense three setter in which she attacked incessantly to take the title. To add to what was an emotional occasion, it was the Queen's Jubilee Year and the Queen herself was there to present the prize.

In 1985, she retired from singles in 1985, but was still playing doubles at Wimbledon up until 1987, aged 42. In all, she competed in a record 26 Wimbledons. Wade also holds the records for the most Federation and Wightman Cup appearances.

Mats Wilander

STATISTICS

Date of Birth: August 22, 1964
Place of Birth: Vaxjo, Sweden
Place of Residence: Greenwich, Connecticut, USA
Nationality: Swedish
Height: 6ft 0in (1.83m)
Plays: Right-handed
Highest Ranking Reached: No. 1 (September 12, 1988)

Career Title Wins
Singles: 33
Doubles: 7

Grand Slam Highlights
Singles
Australian—won 1983, 1984, 1988; runner-up 1985; SF 1990
French—won 1982, 1985, 1988; runner-up 1983, 1987; QF 1989
Wimbledon—QF 1987, 1988, 1989
US—won 1988; runner-up 1987; SF 1985; QF 1983, 1984

Doubles
Australian—runner-up (w/Nystrom) 1984; SF (w/Nystrom) 1985
French—SF (w/Nystrom) 1985
1986—won (w/Nystrom) 1986
US—runner-up (w/Nystrom) 1986; SF (w/Nystrom) 1985

Awards
1985 ATP Tour Sportsmanship Award

The great Mats Wilander began and ended his career in a blaze of newspaper headlines.

The Swede became an overnight star when he won the French Open at the age of just 17, in 1982—just as his compatriot, Bjorn Borg, had retired from the game. Unheralded, Wilander beat the great Guillermo Vilas at his own game, from the baseline, winning 1-6, 7-6 (8-6), 6-0, 6-4.

It was to be the first of seven majors, for although he started off as a typically Swedish topspin baseline player who favoured clay courts, with a lot of determination and discipline he developed attacking skills (including a good volley) that enabled him to win on other surfaces too. In fact, he and Jimmy Connors are the only two players ever to win majors on three surfaces: grass, hard and clay.

In 1983 and 1984, when it was still played at Kooyang on grass, he won the Australian Open; and in 1985, he once again captured the French. 1988, however, was when Wilander peaked, claiming three Grand Slam titles and becoming only the seventh player ever to hold the No. 1 ranking.

The only major he failed to win that year (and, indeed, ever) was Wimbledon, losing to the Czech Miloslav Mecir in the quarter-finals. Ironically, the only Grand Slam doubles title he captured was Wimbledon (with compatriot Joakim Nystrom).

In 1989, having reached the top spot in the world, Wilander appeared to lose motivation and he soon dropped out of the top ten. Then, in 1991, he underwent knee surgery and did not play for two years. In 1994, his first full year on the Tour since 1990, he reached the fourth round at the Australian Open and jumped 200 ranking places.

In 1996, Wilander and Karel Novacek (with whom he had formed quite a successful doubles team) tested positive for cocaine. Both players denied drugs abuse and appealed to the sport's governing body, but the test was upheld. Wilander has not played on the Tour since.

Venus & Serena Williams

STATISTICS

VENUS
Date of Birth: June 17, 1980
Place of Birth: Lynwood, California, USA
Place of Residence: Palm Beach
Gardens, Florida, USA
Nationality: US
Height: 6ft 1.5in (1.86 m)
Plays: Right-handed
Highest Ranking Reached: No. 22
(November 24, 1997)

Grand Slam Highlights
Singles
US—runner-up 1997

Awards
WTA Tour Most Impressive Newcomer
1997

SERENA
Date of Birth: September 26, 1981
Place of Birth: Saginaw, Michigan, USA
Place of Residence: Palm Beach Gardens,
Florida, USA
Nationality: US
Height: 5ft 10in (1.78 m)
Plays: Right-handed
Highest Ranking Reached: No. 99
(November 24, 1997)

Sisters Venus and Serena Williams are two of the most exciting prospects on the women's Tour. Venus, the elder by 15 months, started playing tennis at the age of four and a half. In 1994, at 14, she turned professional to beat the Tour's age restriction requirements.

In her first professional match, at the Oakland event in 1994, Venus beat the American Shaun Stafford (ranked No. 59) in straight sets. In the following round, she fell to world No. 2 Arantxa Sanchez Vicario in three sets, having held a 6-3, 3-0 lead.

Since then, although she still does not play a full tournament schedule, she has made her way up the rankings in leaps and bounds. By April 1997, she had cracked the top 100, helped in only her 24th match as a professional by her first win over a top ten player, Croatia's Iva Majoli, ranked No. 9.

At the 1997 US Open, Venus became the first woman to reach the final in her debut since American Pam Shriver in 1978 and the first unseeded finalist at the US Open since 1958. The final between 16-year old Venus and 17-year old Martina Hingis was the youngest Grand Slam final in the open era.

Serena was playing tennis before she turned six years old and first appeared on the Tour rankings at No. 453 on October 20, 1997. Within three weeks, she was No. 102 because, in only her second Tour event, she beat two top ten players—Mary Pierce and Monica Seles—to get to the semi-finals. In the same event, she reached the semi-finals of the doubles with Venus but was forced to default with a sprained ankle.

Although Serena is considered by many to be an even better prospect than Venus, it was the older sister who was the victor when the two met for the first time professionally, at the Australian Open 1998.

Woodbridge & Woodforde

STATISTICS

Todd Woodbridge
Date of Birth: April 2, 1971
Place of Birth: Sydney, New South Wales, Australia
Place of Residence: Sydney, New South Wales, Australia and Orlando, Florida, USA
Nationality: Australian
Height: 5ft 10in (1.78m)
Plays: Right-handed
Highest Ranking Reached: Doubles No. 1 (July 6, 1992)

Career Title Wins
Doubles: 51

Mark Woodforde
Date of Birth: September 23, 1965
Place of Birth: Adelaide, South Australia, Australia
Place of Residence: Adelaide, South Australia, Australia and Monte Carlo, Monaco
Nationality: Australian
Height: 6ft 1.5in (1.86m)
Plays: Left-handed
Highest Ranking Reached: Doubles No. 1 (November 16, 1992)

Career Title Wins
Doubles: 52

Grand Slam Highlights
Doubles
Australian—won 1992, 1997
French—runners-up 1997
Wimbledon—won 1993, 1994, 1995, 1996, 1997
US—won 1995, 1996; runners-up 1994

Awards
ATP Tour Doubles Team of the Year 1992, 1995, 1996

The Australians Todd Woodbridge and Mark Woodforde, known universally as 'the Woodies', teamed up in 1991. Woodforde, the elder of the two by six years, had been partnering John McEnroe towards the end of his career and they had won three titles together, including the US Open. When the great star finally decided to quit, he suggested Woodforde look for another doubles partner, 'an Aussie, because you guys understand doubles, and a right-hander'. Todd Woodbridge fitted the description perfectly.

Since then, the Woodies have become the most successful doubles team of the 1990s. They have won nine Grand Slam titles—more than any other pair in the open era. They hold the record for Wimbledon doubles titles, having won five years running (1993-97). They have an amazing 44-8 win-loss record in doubles finals. And, in 1996, they won 12 titles, including two majors and an Olympic gold medal, which is the most a

pairing has won since the great John McEnroe and Peter Fleming won 15 in 1979.

Although the pair resent being called 'doubles specialists' and have both had successful seasons in singles, with Woodforde breaking into the top twenty in 1996 and Woodbridge doing the same the following year, it is in doubles that they have had greater success.

This success has been based on perfect balance within the team: their games and temperaments are ideally matched. Woodforde is a leftie, while Woodbridge plays right-handed; Woodforde, six years older and wiser, reins in Woodbridge's youthful enthusiasm and, occasionally, hot-headed temper.

Some already consider them to be among the best few doubles teams in tennis history and they are young enough (although Woodforde, now in his thirties, is getting old by the game's standards) to have a good two or three years left in them yet.

List of Players